English AHEAD

Grade 4

Janet Bartier • William Young

Printed in China

CONTENTS

Nouns

countable, uncountable

1

In this unit, students will:

- learn what countable nouns and uncountable nouns are, and identify them in a piece of writing.
- learn some expressions with uncountable nouns (e.g. a glass of water).
- understand that some nouns can be countable or uncountable depending on the meaning of the sentence.
- learn to use "few" and "many" with countable nouns, and "little" and "much" with uncountable nouns.
- identify countable and uncountable nouns in a picture and put them into sentences to describe the picture.

A. Read and look at the nouns in bold. Underline the ones that are countable.

To check if a noun is countable, see if it is one of these:

- The noun is plural (e.g. "animals").
- The noun is singular, but there is "a" or "one" in front of it.

Ben: Lou, how many **llamas** do you have at Lou's Llama Land?

Lou: We have six llamas, but we hope to get more. We need to raise about 3000 **dollars** first. We'll be able to keep six or seven more llamas then. Llamas like to have **friends**. They're used to living in a **herd**.

Ben: What do your llamas eat?

Lou: They graze on **grass**, and we feed them **hay**. Llamas aren't picky eaters, and they're not big eaters. Milo, one of the llamas here, likes to eat **apples** as a **treat**.

Ben: What else do they need?

Lou: Llamas need plenty of **water**. They need **daylight** and fresh **air**. They need **land** to run around. Also, llamas need **love** and **attention** just like **horses** do. We and the llamas here are like a **family**.

Ben: What do you get back from your llamas?

Lou: We shear them for their **fur**, which can be used to make **jackets**.

Ben: Is there anything else you get out of having llamas?

Lou: We get **happiness**! Llamas are gentle and friendly **animals**. They're wonderful to have.

B. Read what this llama says and finish the expressions with the uncountable nouns from (A).

1. a lot of ____________
2. a bit of ____________
3. a bundle of ____________
4. a patch of ____________
5. a glass of ____________
6. a stack of ____________
7. a ray of ____________
8. a breath of ____________
9. a bunch of ____________
10. an acre of ____________

Think!

Some nouns can be countable in one sentence but uncountable in another, like the following two nouns. Use each of them correctly in the sentences. Remember to add an "s" if necessary.

1. **room**
   - There are two ____________ in the tree house.
   - There is enough ____________ to fit ten people here!

2. **joy**
   - Pets can bring ____________ to their owners.
   - There are two ____________ in my life: my snake and my lizard.

C. See what words we use for countable and uncountable nouns. Put a check mark for the two correct sentences. Put a cross for the wrong ones and correct them.

Countable Nouns
few, many

too many llamas

Uncountable Nouns
little, much

too little water

1. Lou's wife made too much jackets for him. ______
2. There are too little treats for the llamas today. ______
3. Two apples are too few to share among the llamas. ______
4. "Can there ever be too much love?" Lou asks. ______

Corrections

Question ______ : ________________________________

Question ______ : ________________________________

D. Fill in the blanks with "many", "much", "little", or "few".

1. "How ________ llamas do you have?" Ben asks Lou.
2. Milo was sad today because he got very ________ attention.
3. "How ________ water is there in the barrel?" asks Lou.
4. Our backyard used to have very ________ birds, but there are more now thanks to the bird feeder.

Look at the ingredients and the tools in this picture. List the countable and uncountable nouns. Then put them together in sentences.

Countable Nouns:

- one ____________
- one ____________
- two ____________
- four ____________

Uncountable Nouns:

- a bag of ____________
- a tub of ____________
- a carton of ____________

1. The ingredients that the girls took out for making cookies are ____ ____.

2. The tools that they will use are ________________________ ____ ____.

THINGS TO TRY

- **Look through some newspapers and magazines.**
- **Cut out as many nouns as you can find.**
- **Glue the countable nouns in the "counting jar" and the uncountable nouns outside the jar.**

Checklist

Skills

- [ ] I know what countable nouns and uncountable nouns are, and I can identify them in a piece of writing.
- [ ] I know some expressions with uncountable nouns (e.g. a glass of water).
- [ ] I know that some nouns are countable in one sentence but uncountable in another.
- [ ] I know when to use "many" or "much" and when to use "little" or "few".
- [ ] I can identify countable and uncountable nouns in a picture and put them into sentences to describe the picture.

Revising

- [ ] I have checked my spelling.
- [ ] My uncountable nouns are not in plural form.

Compound Words

words made of smaller words

2

In this unit, students will:

- learn some compound words (e.g. butterfly, ladybug).
- identify compound words in a piece of writing.
- write some compound words using pictures or words.
- break compound words into smaller words.
- identify compound words in a picture and put them into a paragraph to describe the picture.

A. Read and look at the words in bold. Underline the ones that are compound words.

This morning, a **butterfly** slurped all the nectar from the **flowers** in the garden, so the **honeybee** and the **hummingbird** had **nothing** to eat. They had been having **breakfast** in this garden every **day**. Who was this butterfly that came uninvited? Buzzing and humming, they sounded the **alarm**, "Follow that butterfly!"

A **ladybug** heard their **call** and quickly caught up. Then a **grasshopper** leaped to the chase. Even a **bulldog** took part. But **none** of them were as quick as the butterfly.

A boy on **skateboard** joined the **chase**, too, gliding on the **sidewalk**. A **policewoman**, curious about all the commotion, ran after **everybody**, blowing her **whistle**. A **bookkeeper** saw them through his office **window** and followed along. Still, the butterfly flitted through the **city** and **nobody** caught up.

Finally, it stopped to rest on a **tree**. Would the honeybee, the hummingbird, the ladybug, the grasshopper, the bulldog, the boy on skateboard, the policewoman, and the bookkeeper catch the butterfly? When they reached the tree, they looked up and saw **thousands** of beautiful **butterflies** on the branches, getting ready for **migration**. They all got carried away by this amazing **sight**

and completely forgot about the chase – except the honeybee and the hummingbird, who were **hungry** and buzzed over to the nearest **flowerpot** to look for breakfast.

B. Look at the pictures to write compound words. Then write the smaller words of the next two compound words. Finally, write the answers to the butterfly's questions.

1.  ____________

2.  ____________

3.  ____________

4. grasshopper = ____________ + ____________
5. hummingbird = ____________ + ____________
6. What is the compound word from (A) that is...

a. a meal? ____________

b. a place to walk? ____________

c. a container for flowers? ____________

Think!

Write a synonym for each word to find out what the "real" compound words are.

1. Words:  mug +  plank

   Synonyms: ____________ + ____________ = ____________

2. Words:  dirt +  crate

   Synonyms: ____________ + ____________ = ____________

C. Match the words on the left with the words on the right to write compound words. Then make up a sentence using any two of the compound words.

cat	paste
sand	corn
tooth	fish
grand	print
foot	mother
pop	paper

____
____
____
____
____
____

Sentence:

____
____
____

Look for the six compound words in this picture. Write them down and then use them to describe the picture in a paragraph.

Compound Words:

cow ____________

horse ____________

rain ____________

rain ____________

sand ____________

sun ____________

Description:

THINGS TO TRY

- **Use blank pieces of paper to cut out rectangles of this size and draw a line down the middle.**
- **Think of two compound words that share one of the smaller words, write them on separate rectangles, and link them by lining up the same words.**
- **Think of more compound words to continue your chain. Cut out more rectangles as you need.**

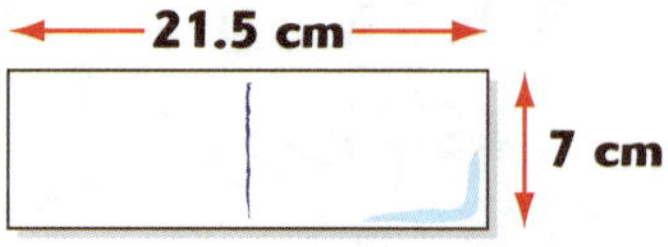

e.g.

| break | fast |
| fast | ball |

e.g.

break	fast
fast	ball
ball	room
base	ball

My Compound Words:

Checklist

Skills

- ☐ I can identify compound words in a piece of writing.
- ☐ I can write some compound words using pictures or words.
- ☐ I can identify the smaller words in a compound word.
- ☐ I can identify compound words in a picture and put them into a paragraph to describe the picture.

Revising

- ☐ I have checked my spelling.
- ☐ My paragraph is in complete sentences.

Verbs

present tense, future tense

3

In this unit, students will:

- identify verbs in the future tense in a piece of writing.
- write sentences in the future tense to answer questions.
- use verbs in the present tense to do a crossword puzzle.
- recognize the tense of a sentence and finish it with a verb in the correct tense.
- know that we can form the future tense using "will" or "going to".
- use the "will" form of future tense to describe some ways of plant seed dispersion.

A. Read Julie's notes from Science class. Check the sentences that have verbs in the future tense.

(A) Ducks waddle on land, but they glide gracefully in and on water.

(B) Tadpoles swish their tails back and forth. When they have their legs and lungs, they will amble out of the pond.

(A) Cheetahs are used to open spaces. When it spots prey, it will stalk and chase it.

(B) Squirrels nimbly climb up trees to find shelter and food.

(A) Moles dig and shovel passageways that lead to secret rooms.

(B) Many insects lay their eggs underground. When the eggs hatch, the insects will tunnel to the surface.

(A) Kingfishers must live near still or slow moving water. There, they fly low and hover, and then dive for their meals.

(B) Bats dart around the night sky. When they find tasty insects, they will snatch them up!

B. Answer these questions with sentences in the future tense.

1. What will tadpoles do when they have legs and lungs?

2. What will bats do when they find tasty insects?

C. Read the clues and complete this crossword puzzle with verbs from (A).

Across

A. How tadpoles move through water
B. How baby insects get to the surface
C. How cheetahs hunt
D. How kingfishers catch their food

Down

1. How ducks move on land
2. How moles make their passageways

D. Think about the tense of each sentence. Finish it with the given verb in the present tense or the future tense.

1. Tomorrow, I ________________ (practise) my recorder in the music room.

2. When Jim and Sara reach the top of the mountain, they ________________ (plant) a flag and take a picture.

3. "This is how I make bread," says Aunt May. "I knead and ________________ (shape) the dough."

4. When summer arrives, Henry ________________ (travel) to Italy to visit his relatives.

5. "I ________________ (dart) around the sky when night falls," thinks Billy the Bat.

Think!

Besides using the word "will" to form the future tense, we can also use "going to". Use these two forms of future tense to rewrite this sentence.

Carly swims five laps around the pool.

- ____
- ____

Describe some ways that plant seeds spread themselves around. Use the given descriptions to finish the sentences. Use "will" to write in the future tense.

- float to their new home
- spin towards the ground to be carried by wind
- come off the plant and hitch a ride
- carry them away

1. 

When the "helicopter seeds" fall from the maple tree, they ____________________ ____________________.

2. When coconuts drop onto water, they ____________________ ____________________.

3. When we blow the "dandelion clock" to separate its tiny seeds, the breeze ____________________.

4. 

When a furry animal brushes by the mimosa, the seed pot bristles of the mimosa ____________________.

THINGS TO TRY

- **Make up some sentences in the present tense.**
- **Say one sentence at a time to a group of friends and ask them to change it to the future tense (get them to raise their hands first).**
- **The quickest person to raise his/her hand and say the sentence correctly in the future tense will get a point.**

Example:

- Billy turns nine years old today.
- ______________________

  ____
- ______________________

  ____
- ______________________

  ____

Checklist

Skills

- [ ] I can identify verbs in the future tense in a piece of writing.
- [ ] I know how to write sentences in the future tense to answer questions.
- [ ] I can finish a crossword puzzle with verbs in the present tense.
- [ ] I can finish different sentences with verbs in the correct tenses.
- [ ] I know how to write the future tense using "will" or "going to".
- [ ] I can use the future tense to describe some ways that plants spread their seeds around.

Revising

- [ ] I have used "will" or "going to" to form the future tense.
- [ ] I have checked my spelling.

Adjectives

comparative, superlative

4

In this unit, students will:

- learn that "more" and "most" are sometimes used to form comparative and superlative adjectives (e.g. "more interesting", "most interesting").
- identify comparative and superlative adjectives in a piece of writing.
- use "er" comparative adjectives in sentences.
- learn how to write the comparative and superlative forms of adjectives that end in "y".
- learn some irregular comparative and superlative adjectives (e.g. better, best).
- use comparative and superlative adjectives to talk about some Canadian provinces and territories.

A. Kevin is telling everyone to visit Canada. Read and use red to underline the comparative adjectives. Use blue to underline the superlative adjectives.

Quebec

"Visit Canada's biggest province at any time of the year. Enjoy the culture and the summer nights in the cities. Or, during the colder months, ski the snowy mountains!"

New Brunswick

"Come and see the highest tides in the world! The Bay of Fundy is a wonder for tourists and locals alike. It may be more amazing than anything you have ever seen!"

Alberta

"Visit Alberta, the most westerly prairie province and the sunniest province in Canada. Hike in the Rockies and dig for ancient dinosaur bones all in one day!"

Prince Edward Island

"PEI is the most rural province of Canada. It is also the smallest. Set against a quiet landscape, everybody on this island is more relaxed. Come here to get away from the hustle and bustle of your busy life."

B. Finish these sentences with the comparative form of the given adjectives.

1. PEI is ____________ than New Brunswick.
   small
2. It is ____________ in Nunavut than in Ontario.
   cold
3. Quebec is much ____________ than New Brunswick.
   big
4. The tides in New Brunswick are ____________ than those in British Columbia.
   high

C. Read what Becky says and write the comparative and superlative forms of each adjective. Then finish each sentence with the correct form.

When an adjective ends in "y", change the "y" to "i" before adding "er" or "est".

1.

	comparative	superlative
a. snowy		
b. busy		
c. sunny		

2. The sun is here. It's ____________ today than yesterday.
3. The top of the mountain is ____________ than the bottom of the mountain.
4. Wendy has been the ____________ one out of all of us since she started taking guitar lessons.

D. Read what Tom says and write the comparative and superlative forms of each adjective. Then finish each sentence with the correct form.

Usually, when an adjective has two or more syllables, we write "more" or "most" in front of it to make the comparative or superlative form.

1.

	comparative	superlative
a. beautiful		
b. westerly		
c. ancient		
d. rural		

2. Ann chose to live in the ______________ town in the province.

3. Brad thinks that the ______________ cities are in Quebec.

4. Saskatchewan is to the east of Alberta, so Alberta is ______________ than Saskatchewan.

5. "I want to see a city from long ago. Where can I find the world's ______________ city?" asks my brother.

Think!

Some adjectives have irregular comparative and superlative forms. Fill in the blanks.

1. Good is to better as bad is to ______________ .
2. Better is to best as more is to ______________ .

Use the following adjectives in the comparative or superlative form to talk about the given provinces and territories. Look at the map of Canada to do the exercise.

Comparative

1. **small**: Nova Scotia (NS), Prince Edward Island (PEI)

   ____

2. **big**: Nunavut (NU), Manitoba (MB)

   ____

   ____

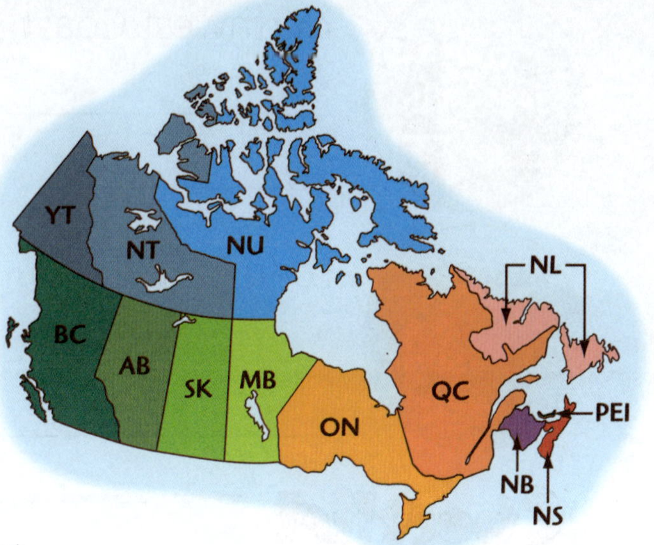

3. **wide**: Ontario (ON), British Columbia (BC)

   ____

   ____

4. **narrow**: Alberta (AB), Saskatchewan (SK)

   ____

Superlative

5. **westerly**: Yukon (YT)

   ____

6. **easterly**: Newfoundland and Labrador (NL)

   ____

THINGS TO TRY

- Pretend you are on the radio to talk about the following places in Canada.
- Use one form of adjective (positive, comparative, or superlative) to write a description for each place.
- Read the descriptions and get a friend to record them for you. Then play them back for fun!

Churchill, Manitoba

" ______________________________

______________________________ "

Northwest Coast, British Columbia

" ______________________________

______________________________ "

Long Range Mountains, Newfoundland and Labrador

" ______________________________

______________________________ "

Checklist

Skills

- ☐ I know when to use "more" and "most" to form comparative and superlative adjectives.
- ☐ I can identify comparative and superlative adjectives in a piece of writing.
- ☐ I know how to use "er" comparative adjectives in sentences.
- ☐ I know how to write the comparative and superlative forms of adjectives that end in "y".
- ☐ I know some irregular comparative and superlative adjectives.
- ☐ I know how to use comparative and superlative adjectives to talk about some Canadian provinces and territories.

Revising

- ☐ I have checked the spelling of my adjectives, especially the comparatives with "ier" and the superlatives with "iest".

Adverbs

words that describe verbs

5

Missy **busily** tidies up her room. She **quickly** shelves her books and puts her clothes **neatly** into her drawer.

In this unit, students will:

- identify "ly" adverbs in a piece of writing.
- use "ly" adverbs in complete sentences to answer questions.
- write the opposite of some "ly" adverbs.
- use a thesaurus to find synonyms for "happily".
- form "ly" adverbs out of adjectives and use them to complete sentences.
- describe a picture using verbs and "ly" adverbs.

A. Read and underline all the "ly" adverbs.

Missy is a pleasant kid. She speaks politely, does her homework diligently, and happily sets the table at dinner time. She could be every parent's dream – except, she doesn't clean her room.

"Why don't you take some time to clean it?" her parents ask one day.

But Missy's room gets messier and messier. Her parents can never find the floor in her room. Missy can never find it either, but she doesn't mind.

One day, her parents can't see their daughter in the room. "Missy!" they call from outside her door. "You're lost in your room! You'd better tidy it up immediately!"

Missy has never heard her parents speak this urgently, which is very unusual. But without a hurry, she wisely answers them, "I will."

Missy gets down to work. She folds her clothes neatly. She busily puts away her books. She makes her bed with freshly washed sheets, tightly tucking in every corner. Then, proudly, Missy calls to her parents downstairs, "My room is now as clean as ever! Come and take a look!"

Her parents eagerly climb up the stairs, but slowly walk down the hall. When they get to Missy's room, they look in suspiciously. "Wow!" they exclaim. Missy's room has completely transformed!

Now, if only Missy could keep it up...

B. Answer these questions in complete sentences.

1. How does Missy do her homework?

____

2. How do Missy's parents climb up the stairs?

____

3. How has Missy's room transformed?

____

C. Write an "ly" adverb that is the opposite of each of these.

1. slowly ______________   2. tightly ______________

3. politely ______________   4. urgently ______________

Think!

A thesaurus is useful when we want to look for synonyms or antonyms. Look in a thesaurus to write the synonyms for "happily". Then complete the sentence with one of the synonyms.

happily: ______________________________

____

____

Missy lives ______________ .

D. Change each adjective into an "ly" adverb. Then use the adverbs to finish the sentences.

Remember: if the adjective ends in "y", change it to "i" before adding "ly".

1. brave ____________ careful ____________
   easy ____________ awkward ____________
   sloppy ____________ wonderful ____________
   cheery ____________ careless ____________

2. After a month of practice, Mike can now ____________ run many laps around the track.

3. Karen is not afraid of heights. She ____________ dives into the pool from the platform.

4. Ben spent hours ____________ making his wooden dinosaur, but his dad ____________ stepped on it!

5. Even though the choir sang ____________, the dancers performed so ____________ that they ruined the show!

6. Mr. Brown is walking very ____________ with a new mop and bags of toilet paper, but he is whistling ____________ down the street.

Your Turn

Look at the people and the animals in this picture. What verbs and "ly" adverbs can you use to describe them? Write them down. Then put them into sentences to make a paragraph.

Verb	Adverb
talking	loudly
singing	happily

THINGS TO TRY

- **Make a list of some funny actions.**
- **Make a list of "ly" adverbs. Think of as many as you can.**
- **Get a group of friends and decide who is the "actor".**
- **The "actor" picks an action and tells the others what it is.**
- **The others take turns calling out an adverb from the list, and the actor must do the action according to the adverb.**
- **When someone calls out an adverb that the actor cannot "act out", then it is that person's turn to be the actor.**

Actions

- *jump sideways*
- *touch the back of your head with your left hand and the bottom of your left foot with your right hand*

Adverbs

- *quickly*
- *cheerily*

Checklist

Skills

- ☐ I can identify "ly" adverbs in a piece of writing.
- ☐ I can use "ly" adverbs in complete sentences to answer questions.
- ☐ I know the opposite of some "ly" adverbs.
- ☐ I know how to find synonyms for "happily" using a thesaurus.
- ☐ I know how to form "ly" adverbs out of adjectives and use them to complete sentences.
- ☐ I can describe a picture using verbs and "ly" dverbs.

Revising

- ☐ I have checked the spelling of my "ly" adverbs, especially the ones formed out of adjectives that end in "y".
- ☐ I have used a suitable "ly" adverb to describe each of my verbs.

Prepositions

words to tell place, direction, time

6

In this unit, students will:

- identify prepositions of place (e.g. inside), direction (e.g. into), and time (e.g. within) in a piece of writing.
- answer questions using prepositions of place, direction, and time.
- learn that "in", "on", and "at" can function as prepositions of place and prepositions of time.
- use prepositions to finish a diary entry.
- describe a picture using prepositions.

A. Read Fifer's message and write "place", "direction", or "time" for each preposition.

I am writing this message **from** a deserted island **in** the Pacific Ocean, where my dog Jake and I have been stranded **since** July 8, 1900. **On** this day, my ship, Lucky Lady, was not lucky at all. **During** a severe thunderstorm, she was filled with water and sank **near** this island. Fortunately, the storm lasted **for** only a few minutes. Jake and I swam and reached the shore **within** hours of the sinking. We're still very exhausted.

1. ______
2. ______
3. ______
4. ______
5. ______
6. ______
7. ______
8. ______

After writing this letter, I will roll it up and put it **inside** a bottle. I'll hurl the bottle **into** the ocean and hope it will drift with the currents **to** a shore.

9. ______
10. ______
11. ______
12. ______

The sun shines hot **in** the day here, but Jake and I shiver **at** night. Please help us soon.

13. ______
14. ______

Gratefully yours,
Fifer

B. Match these answers with the questions. Write the letters.

- A **near** a deserted island in the Pacific Ocean
- B **from** a deserted island in the Pacific Ocean
- C **during** a severe thunderstorm
- D **for** several minutes
- E **since** July 8, 1900
- F **inside** a bottle

1. Where did Fifer's message come from? ____
2. Where did Fifer's ship sink? ____
3. When did Fifer's ship sink? ____
4. Since when has Fifer been stranded? ____
5. How long did the thunderstorm last? ____
6. Where did Fifer put his letter? ____

C. Answer these questions in complete sentences.

1. How soon did Fifer reach the shore?

____

2. Where did Fifer hurl the bottle?

____

Think!

The prepositions "in", "on", and "at" can function as prepositions of place and prepositions of time. Look at the two uses of each one below and write "place" or "time". Then make up two sentences with "at" and do the same thing.

In • The island is in the Pacific Ocean. ____________

• The sun shines in the day. ____________

On • Fifer was on his ship. ____________

• His ship sank on July 8, 1900. ____________

At • ______________________________ ____________

• ______________________________ ____________

D. Fifer wrote in his diary after the rescue. Fill in the blanks to help him finish it.

to
for
from
into
outside
within
near

I had been stranded 1. ____________ a week when a rescue ship sailed 2. ____________ the island. I was 3. ____________ my shelter when I heard the horn, and started a fire 4. ____________ minutes. The ship's crew saw my fire and threw a lifesaver 5. ____________ the water so that I could swim 6. ____________ the ship 7. ____________ the shore.

Your Turn

Look at the picture and write different sentences using the given prepositions and details.

- since ; four o'clock
- for ; 15 minutes
- on ; timer
- to ; Mike
- inside ; basket
- outside ; three-point arc
- during ; cheers

1. ______________________________

2. ______________________________

3. ______________________________

4. ______________________________

5. ______________________________

6. ______________________________

7. ______________________________

THINGS TO TRY

Use prepositions to make a short poem!

- **Write down some imaginary places.**
- **Write down some prepositions of place and prepositions of time.**
- **Put your prepositions and imaginary places together to tell where you want to go and when.**

Imaginary Places:
spaceship haunted house

Prepositions of Place:
inside through

Prepositions of Time:
at in

Let's go...

______________ a spaceship

______________ the earliest hour

______________ a haunted house

______________ the middle of the night

____

____

Checklist

Skills

- ☐ I can identify prepositions of place, direction, and time in a piece of writing.
- ☐ I know how to answer questions using prepositions of place, direction, and time.
- ☐ I know that "in", "on", and "at" can function as prepositions of place and prepositions of time.
- ☐ I can use prepositions to finish a diary entry.
- ☐ I can describe a picture using prepositions.

Revising

- ☐ I have checked my spelling.
- ☐ My sentences begin with a capital letter and end with a period, a question mark, or an exclamation mark.

Conjunctions

connecting words

7

In this unit, students will:

- identify the conjunctions "because", "if", "so", "until", "since", "while", and "although" and understand their meanings by combining sentences.
- learn that some conjunctions can go at the beginning or in the middle of the sentence (e.g. if, although, since).
- use different conjunctions to write different sentence endings.

A. Read and underline these conjunctions.

because so if until
since while although

If you are interested in dinosaurs, take a close look at a rock or two. Only rocks and minerals carry traces of dinosaurs because all living things decompose. These traces found in rocks and minerals are called "fossils".

Here's how fossils are formed: an animal's dead body sinks into a muddy riverbank, and layers upon layers of mud buries it over time. Since the minerals that form rock are also in the water, minerals seep into holes in the buried animal bones. The remains become less and less bone, and more and more minerals. Eventually, the minerals harden until they completely become rocks.

Often, fossil hunters find an imprint – or a "stamp" – of a dinosaur, which could be a footprint. A footprint can tell us a lot about the animal, so it is as exciting as finding a dinosaur bone. Some fossil hunters find fossilized dinosaur eggs, while others discover teeth, or even coprolites. "What are coprolites?" you might ask. It is another word for fossilized dung.

Although fossils of one kind or another can be common, dinosaur fossils are quite rare. In fact, the majority of dinosaurs did not leave behind a fossil. If you live where dinosaurs used to roam, and where there is rock formed from mud that is millions of years old, you might be able to find a dinosaur fossil.

B. Finish the sentences with the given choices.

- **until** they are as hard as rocks
- **while** others find dinosaur teeth or dung
- **because** we can learn a lot from footprints

1. Some fossil hunters find fossilized dinosaur eggs, ____.

2. Eventually, the minerals harden ____.

3. Finding a footprint is as exciting as finding a dinosaur bone ____.

Think!

For each sentence, switch the underlined parts, take away the comma, and replace "so" with a different conjunction without changing the meaning of the sentence.

1. Janet has never seen a dinosaur fossil, so she is excited to find a dinosaur head.

   ____

   ____

2. Janet and Bill have finished their work today, so they are going home.

   ____

   ____

C. Read what Janet says. Rewrite each sentence so that the conjunction is in the middle of the sentence.

Some conjunctions can go at the beginning or in the middle of the sentence, depending on which part of the sentence you write first.

1. **If** you are interested in dinosaurs, take a close look at a rock or two.

   Take a close look at a rock or two if ________________

   ____

2. **If** you live where dinosaurs used to roam, you might be able to find a dinosaur fossil.

   ____

   ____

3. **Although** fossils of one kind or another can be common, dinosaur fossils are quite rare.

   ____

   ____

4. **Since** the minerals that form rock are also in the water, minerals seep into holes in the buried animal bones.

   ____

   ____

   ____

Make a list of all the conjunctions you know. Then use them to write endings for these sentences. Use each conjunction only once.

Conjunctions

1. I will wear my orange striped socks

____

___________________________________ .

2. Jack and Jill are coming to visit

____

___________________________________ .

3. Austin wants to join the baseball team

____

___________________________________ .

4. Ben and Jerry rollerbladed to the park

____

___________________________________ .

5. Carrie is harvesting apples in the orchard

____

___________________________________ .

THINGS TO TRY

- **On separate cue cards, use a marker to write down all the conjunctions you know.**
- **On some cue cards, write down two conjunctions.**
- **Put the cards in a box and shuffle.**
- **With two or three friends, take turns drawing a card from the box. Make a sentence with the conjunction you get.**
- **The one who draws a card with two conjunctions has to make a sentence containing both conjunctions.**
- **Take turns making sentences until the box is empty.**

Conjunctions:

______________ ______________

______________ ______________

______________ ______________

______________ ______________

______________ ______________

Cue cards:

Checklist

Skills

- ☐ I can identify the conjunctions "because", "if", "so", "until", "since", "while", and "although" and understand their meanings.
- ☐ I know that "if", "although", and "since" can go at the beginning or in the middle of the sentence.
- ☐ I know how to use different conjunctions to write different sentence endings.

Revising

- ☐ I have put a comma before "so", but not before "because".
- ☐ My sentences begin with a capital letter and end with a period, a question mark, or an exclamation mark.

Sentences

simple, compound, complex

8

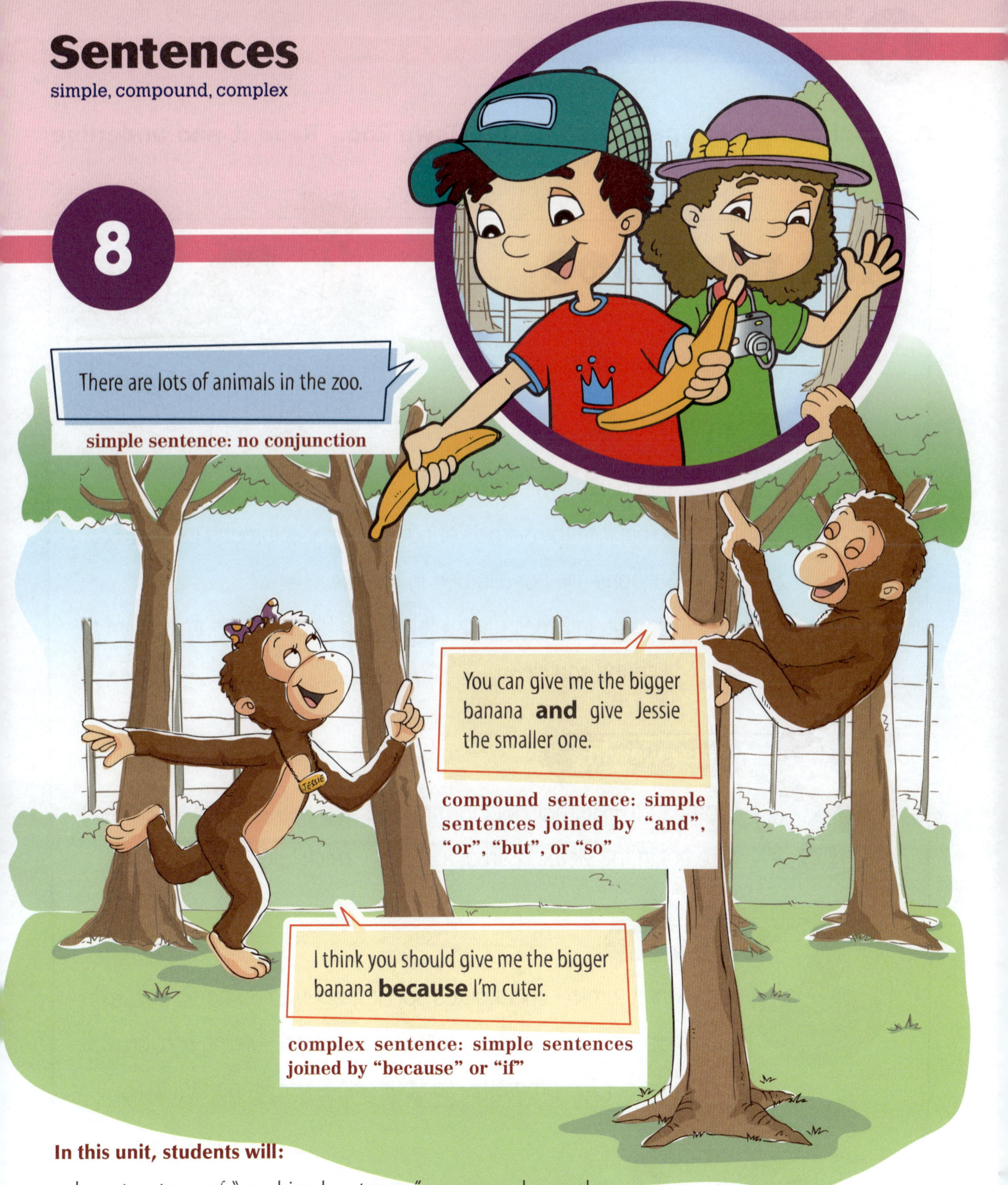

In this unit, students will:

- learn two types of "combined sentences": compound, complex.
- identify conjunctions in a pamphlet (coordinating: and, or, but, so; subordinating: because, if).
- identify simple, compound, and complex sentences in the pamphlet.
- know that a compound sentence must have at least two simple sentences.
- use conjunctions to combine simple sentences.
- use compound and complex sentences to describe what is going on in a picture.

A. Jodi designed a pamphlet for the Town Zoo. Read it and underline all the conjunctions.

THE TOWN ZOO

Opening Hours: Mon – Fri: 9:00 a.m. – 4:00 p.m.
Sat – Sun: 10:00 a.m. – 5:00 p.m.

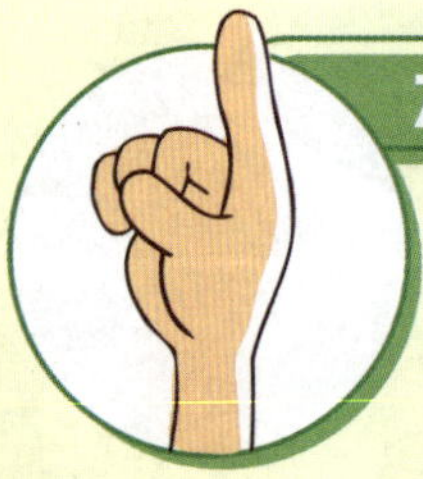

Zoo Rules

1. Stay behind the yellow line.
2. Do not feed the animals or put your fingers through the fences.
3. Balloons are not allowed in the zoo.
4. Eat only in areas with a  sign because it is important to keep the zoo clean.

Animal Viewing

Some of the animals take a mid-day nap in their shelters. If they are not in the viewing area, just come back later.

Donations

We want to protect endangered species, but we can do so only with your help. Your donations will go toward habitat rebuilding and they will help fund our zoo programs, so your help is very important to us.

Parking

All zoo visitors park for free. Free parking is for zoo visitors only. If you want to park your car and then use the nearby subway, you should use the pay parking lot beside the subway station.

B. Use Jodi's pamphlet to complete this activity.

1. Find a simple sentence from the pamphlet.

   ____

2. Which zoo rule is a compound sentence?

   _____ ; coordinating conjunction: _____

3. Which zoo rule is a complex sentence?

   _____ ; subordinating conjunction: _____

4. Find the compound sentence with two coordinating conjunctions.

   ____

   ____

Think!

In every compound sentence, there are at least two simple sentences. If there's only one, then it's not a compound sentence. Write "compound" for the compound sentences below.

1. Park at the East Lot or park at the West Lot. __________
2. Park at the east lot or the west lot. __________
3. This is Jodi's first visit but Michael's ninth. __________
4. This is Jodi's first visit but it's Michael's ninth. __________

C. Combine the given sentences using a conjunction that makes sense for the new sentence. Then write "compound" or "complex" to tell what kind of sentence you made.

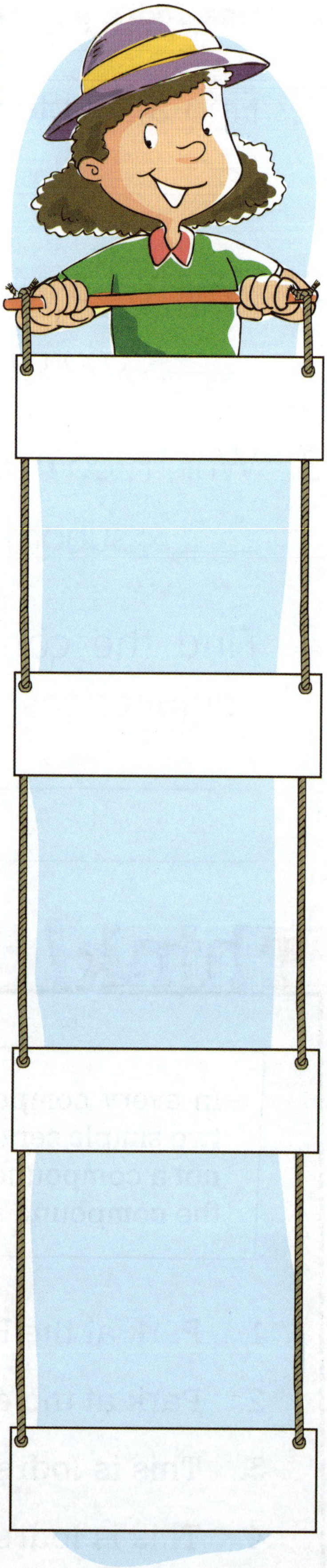

1. Michael wants to see the boa constrictor.
   He loves all kinds of reptiles.

   ____

   ____

2. Dave is down with a cold.
   He can't go to see the zebras.

   ____

   ____

3. Mrs. Lee bought a zoo pass.
   She can take her kids to the zoo every week this summer.

   ____

   ____

4. Jodi loves animals.
   She wants to make a donation.
   The zoo is closed for a month.

   ____

   ____

Look what each person is doing. Use the given conjunction for each person to write a sentence about each one.

1. ______________________________

2. ______________________________

3. ______________________________

4. ______________________________

5. ______________________________

6. ______________________________

THINGS TO TRY

Use different types of sentences to explain how to make an omelette! Follow our instructions.

How to Make an Omelette

Type	Words to Include
1. **compound**:	crack, eggs, and, beat, bowl
2. **simple**:	add, pieces, ham
3. **compound**:	put, microwave, and, heat, one minute
4. **complex**:	overheat, because, dry
5. **compound**:	take, microwave, enjoy, omelette

1. Crack two eggs and beat them in a bowl.

2. ______________________________

3. ______________________________

4. ______________________________

5. ______________________________

Checklist

Skills

- ☐ I know what compound sentences and complex sentences are.
- ☐ I can identify conjunctions and different types of sentences in a pamphlet.
- ☐ I know that a compound sentence must have at least two simple sentences.
- ☐ I know how to combine simple sentences using conjunctions.
- ☐ I can describe what is going on in a picture using compound and complex sentences.

Revising

- ☐ I have written in complete sentences.
- ☐ I have a comma before "so", but not before "because".

Punctuation

putting them all together

9

The knights asked, "How can that be possible? You're only a newt!"

, comma:
to show a pause before starting direct speech

" " quotation marks:
to show direct speech

' apostrophe:
to form the contraction of "you are"

In this unit, students will:

- learn another use of the comma: to show a pause before direct speech.
- put in missing commas, quotation marks, and apostrophes.
- learn some examples of indirect speech and match them with sentences of direct speech.
- learn that the same words can be expressed differently with different punctuation marks.
- change indirect speech to direct speech using correct punctuation.

A. Put the following punctuation marks in the coloured patches.

,   “   ”   ’

In the time of kings and castles, it was common for a boy to dream of becoming a knight. The trouble with Norman, who wanted to be a knight, was that he wasn t a boy. Norman was a newt.

Norman scrabbled to a castle near the pond where he was born. At the gate, he said to the guards I want to be a knight.

How can a newt be a knight? asked one of the guards. A newt lives in the marshes. The guard stomped his foot and called to the others This newt is a nut! Close the gate!

Disappointed, Norman went home. Before long, his wish to be a knight took him back to the castle. This time, he bumped into some knights on their way to a tournament. He said I want to be a knight like you.

One of the knights laughed and said A newt is only a threat to insects and worms, not knights from other kingdoms. The knight raised his sword and said This newt is a hoot! Onward, knights!

Norman would have to go straight to the king. He squeezed under the gate, crawled past the guards, and wriggled up the wall to an open window. What luck! He was in the throne room, and there was the king, polishing his golden crown.

Your Majesty, Norman said quickly before the king could call his guards I want to be a knight. Knights must fight for their king, so I m perfect for the job. After all, I eat *dragon*flies!

The king didn t know much about newts, nor did he know anything about dragonflies, but it certainly sounded brave to eat them. And so, by order of the king, Norman the newt became a knight!

Think!

Each sentence below is an example of "**indirect speech**". Find the sentence containing direct speech in (A) that has the same meaning.

1. He said to the guards at the gate that he wanted to be a knight.

____

2. One of the guards asked how a newt could be a knight.

____

B. Put the missing punctuation marks in these sentences.

1. The guard said "This newt is a nut!"

2. The knight said, This newt is a hoot!

3. The king said This newt is brave!

C. Read what this knight says. Look at each expression and write the same sentence with the correct punctuation mark.

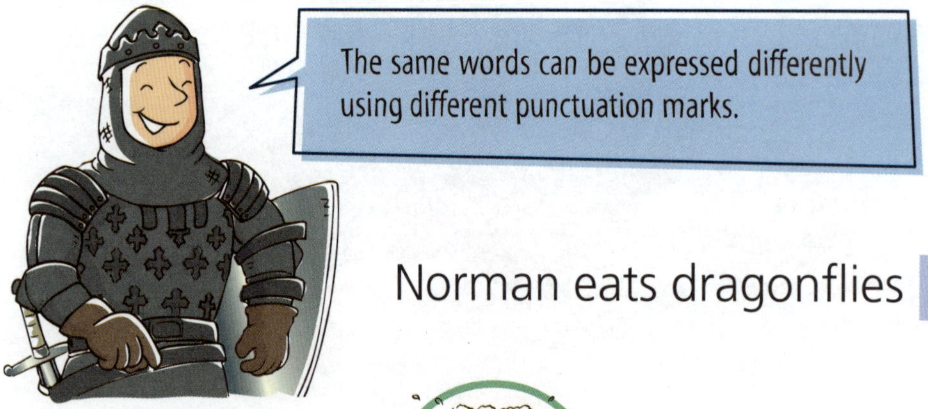

Norman eats dragonflies . ! ?

1. ______________________________

2. ______________________________

3. ______________________________

Your Turn

Read this continuation of the story about Norman. Use the indirect speech to help you think of the direct speech for each character. Remember to use the comma and quotation marks.

After Norman's visit, the king came out of the throne room to announce that the newt would become a knight. His guard asked if he was sure about it. His knight said very calmly that Norman was much smaller than all of them. Then, with determination, Norman exclaimed that he would learn to slay real dragons.

1. The king said ________________________________

2. The guard said ________________________________

3. The knight said ________________________________

4. Norman said ________________________________

THINGS TO TRY

Name	Score in Rounds		
	1st	2nd	3rd

- Write the correct punctuation mark for each use.
- Make six cue cards like the ones below.
- Put the cards face down on a table.
- Ask a parent or older sibling to help you make a score sheet and keep score.
- With a few friends, take turns picking a card. Use all the punctuation marks there to make a sentence. Write it down and read it aloud. A correct sentence gets a point.
- Return each card to the table, face down, and shuffle.

Punctuation Marks

☐ to say a statement

☐ to ask a question

☐ to show strong feeling

☐ to show direct speech

☐ to form contractions

☐ to pause before direct speech

Cue Cards to Make

Checklist

Skills

☐ I know another use of the comma: to show a pause before direct speech.

☐ I know where to put in commas, quotation marks, and apostrophes.

☐ I know what indirect speech is and can match it with direct speech.

☐ I know that different punctuation marks can express the same words differently.

☐ I know how to change indirect speech to direct speech using correct punctuation.

Revising

☐ I have used quotation marks to show direct speech.

☐ I have put a comma before my open quotation marks.

A. Fill in the blanks with the given words to help Andrea finish the summary of her favourite book.

"Have you ever read *Charlotte's Web*? It's a wonderful story by E.B. White that tells how a beautiful grey spider named Charlotte saves the life of a young pig named Wilbur."

Part 1

confidence animals web bedtime himself bacon

Wilbur lives in a barn with other 1. ____________ . He is scared when they tell him that he will eventually be killed and become 2. ____________ on someone's plate, but Charlotte promises to save him by spinning words into her 3. ____________ to make him famous.

Charlotte becomes Wilbur's best friend. She cares for him like a mother, telling him 4. ____________ stories, teaching him manners, and encouraging him when he is down. She builds his 5. ____________ so that one day he can stand up for 6. ____________ . Thanks to Charlotte, the farmer lets Wilbur live and even takes him to the county fair, where he wins a prize.

Part 2

friendship lifespan eggs
loyalty love

At the fair, Charlotte lays a sac of 7. ____________ . A spider's 8. ____________ is short, however, and Charlotte dies before she can return to the barn. To thank Charlotte, Wilbur takes the eggs back to the barn with him, and looks after them until they hatch. This story teaches the value of 9. ____________ , 10. ____________ , and 11. ____________ . It will touch your heart. You might even read it again and again like I did!

B. Answer these questions with your answers from (A).

1. What are the five countable nouns?

____

2. What are the four uncountable nouns?

____

3. What are the four compound words?

____

4. Which two compound words are also countable nouns?

____

C. Fill in the blanks with the future tense of the given verbs. Use "will".

1. Wilbur is scared that he ________________ (die), but his best friend Charlotte ________________ (save) his life. She ________________ (spin) words like "TERRIFIC" and "GREAT" into her web so that the farmer ________________ (want) to keep him.

2. Because Charlotte is wise, she ________________ (guide) Wilbur like a teacher. When Wilbur gets older, he ________________ (be) able to take care of himself.

3. Now that Wilbur is famous, the farmer ________________ (take) him to the county fair, where Wilbur ________________ (win) a prize.

4. Charlotte is dying, but Wilbur ________________ (return) to the barn with her sac of eggs and he ________________ (look after) them until they hatch.

5. What do you think will happen when Charlotte's eggs hatch at the barn? Write down your predictions using the future tense.

____

____

____

REVIEW

D. Fill in the blanks with the comparative form, the superlative form, or the adverb made from each given adjective.

1. **kind**

Charlotte is the ____________ (superlative) animal in the barn. She talks to Wilbur ____________ (adverb).

2. **patient**

Charlotte is the ____________ (superlative) of all the animals. She thinks ____________ (adverb) for a good idea that will help Wilbur live.

3. **busy**

Charlotte is ____________ (comparative) now than before. Besides catching flies, she ____________ (adverb) spins words of praise for Wilbur into her web.

4. **independent**

Wilbur needs to become ____________ (comparative) in the future. That is why Charlotte helps him build his confidence so that when he grows up, he will live ____________ (adverb).

E. Look at this picture and finish the description with the given prepositions.

Charlotte and Wilbur are 1. ______________ a hut. They have been there 2. ______________ four o'clock in the afternoon. They are going to meet up with their new friends 3. ______________ sunset. A mother cow and her two little kids are standing 4. ______________ the hut, which is 5. ______________ an apple tree. There is a squirrel jumping very happily 6. ______________ the tree 7. ______________ the roof of the hut. He will play with his friends 8. ______________ eating his apple.

REVIEW

F. Use the given conjunctions to make two compound sentences and two complex sentences. Then tell which sentences are compound and which ones are complex.

and or but so because if

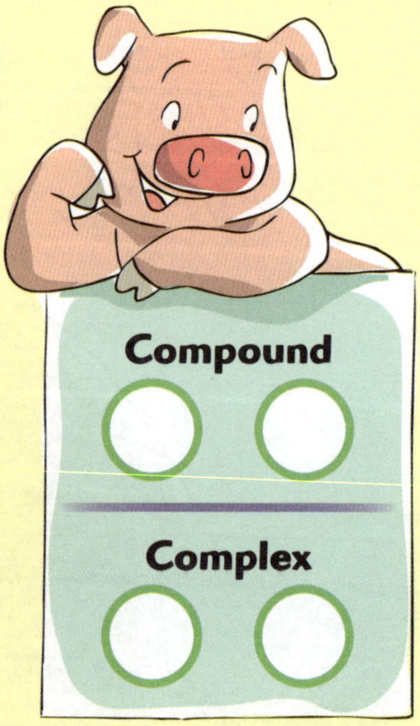

1. Wilbur and his friends went out to play ______________________ ______________________.

2. Benjamin wants to visit the farm ______________________ ______________________.

3. Charlotte will spin a word for the rat ______________________ ______________________.

4. Michael will sleep over at the barn ______________________ ______________________.

G. Put in the missing comma, two missing apostrophes, and the missing quotation marks in the following.

Shortly before Charlotte dies at the county fair, she says to Wilbur A spiders life cant help being something of a mess, with all the trapping and catching flies. By helping you, perhaps I was trying to lift up my life a trifle.

Theme

the author's message in a story

10

In this unit, students will:

- understand that "theme" is the main message of a story.
- identify the theme of a story.
- use the correct verbs to finish a summary of the story.
- recall the details that support the theme of the story.
- connect the story to their own experiences.
- make up a story with a given theme.

A. Read this story. Then check the sentence that is the theme of the story.

Sophie and the Necklace

The necklace was lying on the sidewalk near her school like it was waiting for someone. When Sophie saw it, the gold chain sparkled and shimmered like it was smiling, so she stooped to pick it up.

At a store window, Sophie glanced to see how the necklace shone against her purple T-shirt. It seemed to rest so happily around her neck. It was as though the necklace had found her. When Sophie saw a fashionable woman walking up to her, she was worried that the woman might be looking for it, so she tucked the necklace under her shirt.

"Could you tell me how to get to the theatre?" the woman asked. Sophie gave the directions, and sighed in relief. The woman was not looking for the necklace.

Sophie had just pulled the necklace back out when she noticed a well-dressed man searching his pockets. Holding her breath, she covered the gold chain with her hands. The man took out a quarter and put it in the parking meter. Sophie breathed out. The man was not looking for the necklace.

Then Sophie thought about the woman and the man. They weren't looking for any missing jewellery, but somebody, somewhere, must be. Sophie unclasped the necklace from her neck and looked at it. The necklace glinted back. She put it in her pocket and skipped home, smiling. She would write a "NECKLACE FOUND" ad and put it in the newspaper.

Theme:

Ⓐ All that glitters is gold.

Ⓑ We should always be honest.

Ⓒ Leave your valuables at home.

B. Fill in the blanks with the given verbs to finish the summary of the story.

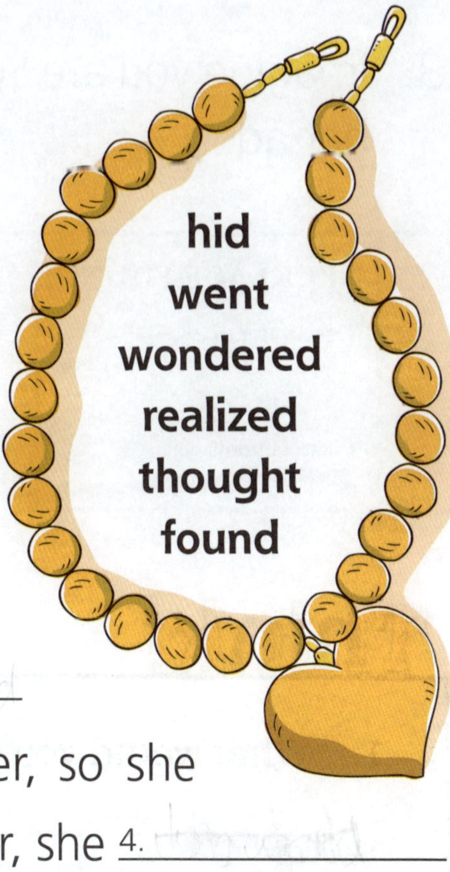

Sophie 1. ____________ a necklace on the sidewalk. When she saw a fashionable woman, she 2. ____________ that the necklace might belong to her, so she 3. ___hid___ it under her shirt. Later, she 4. ____________ if the necklace might belong to a man searching his pockets. Eventually, Sophie 5. ___realized___ that someone must be looking for the necklace, so she 6. ___went___ home to write a "FOUND" ad.

C. Write in your own words and in complete sentences.

1. Why did Sophie unclasp the necklace from her neck?

____

2. How did Sophie feel about her decision in the end? How do we know this?

____

____

3. Imagine you are Sophie. Finish writing her ad.

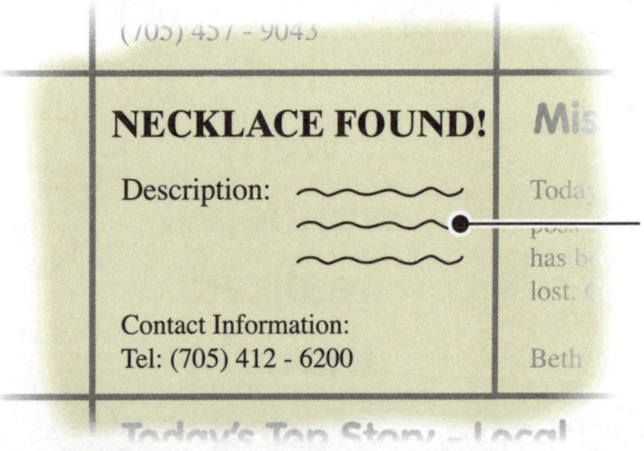

____

____

____

Think!

1. **What would you do if you found something valuable?**

____

____

2. **What would you do if you lost something valuable?**

____

____

Make up a story like "Sophie and the Necklace" that deals with the theme of honesty. Write down the details and draw a picture of the "found item" first. Remember to give your story a title.

Found item: ______________________

Location: ______________________

Characters

main: ______________________

supporting: 1. ______________________

2. ______________________

Search "tool"
(ad, notice, etc.): ______________________

____

____

____

____

____

____

____

____

____

THINGS TO TRY

- **Write down the title of your favourite book and make a simple sketch of its cover.**
- **Think about its theme and write it down. It could be a word (e.g. love, friendship) or a sentence (e.g. Make new friends, but keep the old.)**
- **Brainstorm some things related to the theme: words, stories, and songs.**

Theme: ______________________

____

Things related to the theme:

- Words: ______________________

____

- Stories: ______________________

____

- Songs: ______________________

____

Checklist

Skills

- ☐ I know that "theme" is the main message of a story.
- ☐ I can identify the theme of a story.
- ☐ I can use the correct verbs to finish a summary of the story.
- ☐ I can recall details that support the theme of the story.
- ☐ I can connect the story to my own experiences.
- ☐ I know how to make up a story using a given theme.

Revising

- ☐ I have checked my spelling.
- ☐ I have written in complete sentences.

Setting

What do you see, hear, smell, taste, and feel?

11

Setting:

- bats squeaking (hear)
- a broken window (see)
- chills in the air (feel)

In this unit, students will:

- identify the place, season, and time of day of a story.
- identify details of a "spooky" setting.
- tell whether they can "see", "hear", "smell", "taste", or "feel" the different details of a story's setting.
- write a paragraph to describe an imaginary haunted house.

A. Read this story. Then answer each question in a complete sentence and write the correct clue sentence in blue that gave you the answer.

A House for Halloween

George and Marcus shuffled through fallen leaves on their way home. Halloween was coming up and they wanted to do a scary project.

"How about a haunted house?" Marcus asked, shading his eyes from the late afternoon sun.

"That's old," replied George, bored. "We need something scarier than our graveyard model from last year. The boys now reached their tree-lined street of comfortable homes. In winter, chimneys puffed out the sweet smoke of burning wood while families ate roasted marshmallows. It was hard to imagine any one of them being scary. But suddenly, George said, "Unless..."

Marcus followed George's gaze. He was looking at the Wilson House.

"No one lives there anymore," George spoke faster. "I've seen bats come and go from the attic. They squeak as they fly. Imagine turning the Wilson House into our haunted house!"

The attic had a broken window. The house was strangely dark against the clear blue sky. It had a roof so pointed that it seemed to pierce the sky. There were two dead trees with bare branches. This house was very spooky, and gave Marcus the chills.

"Let's meet in front of the house tonight!" George said, excited. "If we could find a way to get inside, we could start working on our haunted house!"

Except, Marcus wasn't so sure about this idea anymore...

1. Where did the story take place, in busy downtown, or in a quiet neighbourhood?

____

____

2. In which season did the story take place?

____

____

3. What time of day was it?

____

____

Think!

The Wilson House is a spooky setting. Look at the sixth paragraph and list four details about this house and its surroundings that make it spooky.

- ____
- ____
- ____
- ____

B. Fill in the blanks to finish these details of the setting. Then write down whether you can "see", "hear", "smell", "taste", or "feel" them.

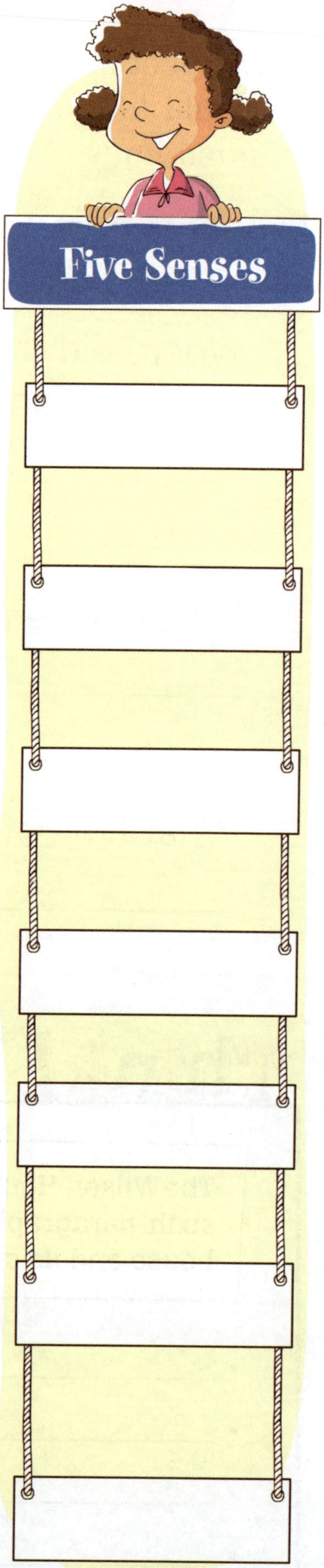

Details

1. George and Marcus __________ through fallen leaves on their way home.

2. The chimneys puffed out the __________ smoke of burning wood in winter.

3. Families ate __________ marshmallows in winter.

4. George has seen __________ fly in and out of the Wilson House.

5. The bats __________ as they fly.

6. The Wilson House had an attic with a __________ window, a __________ roof, and two __________ trees.

7. The Wilson House gave Marcus the __________ .

Your Turn

Imagine you are George or Marcus. You have finished decorating your haunted house. Describe the setting. Plan out your details first. Then write a paragraph.

Details about the Wilson House

Where: inside / outside the house

When: early / late evening

What do you...

see?

hear?

smell?

taste?

feel?

Description

___

___

___

___

___

BOOKS TO READ

Title:
The Tale of Despereaux

Author:
Kate Dicamillo

Publisher:
Candlewick Press (2003)

Leo's Rating: ★★★★★

"This story takes place in a castle. A very tiny mouse named Despereaux falls in love with a princess, but is thrown into the dark dungeon. He must find a way back to the light of the castle and save the princess. The use of 'light' and 'dark' in this story is very interesting."

Title:
The Several Lives of Orphan Jack

Author:
Sarah Ellis

Publisher:
Groundwood Books (2003)

Marie's Rating: ★★★★½

"Jack is a 12-year-old orphan in the Opportunities School for Orphans and Foundlings, but his 'opportunity' to become a 'bookkeeper' turned out to be a disaster. He decided to leave the stifling orphanage for a village by the open sea. This change in setting lets us see the journey through Jack's eyes."

Checklist

Skills

- ☐ I can identify the place, season, and time of day of a story.
- ☐ I can identify the details of a "spooky" setting.
- ☐ I can "see", "hear", "smell", "taste", and "feel" the different details of a story's setting.
- ☐ I can write a paragraph to describe an imaginary haunted house.

Revising

- ☐ I have checked my spelling.
- ☐ I have written in complete sentences.

Characters

A story can have two main characters!

12

In this unit, students will:

- identify the two main characters of a story.
- learn more about the two main characters through Q & A.
- understand the meaning of "rivals".
- identify the reasons that cause the changes in the two main characters.
- create a rival of an imaginary monster and describe how they change from being rivals to being partners.

A. Read this story and answer the questions in complete sentences.

A Clown Too Many

Merry stepped into her new shoes and shook each foot. The bells at the tip of her colourful, upturned shoes jingled. These will make the kids laugh, she thought. She had been looking for something to add to her clown act ever since Hairy joined the circus. She had always been the only clown, but now she shared the spotlight, and the applause, with Hairy.

Later that night, Merry jingled her bells between bows. The children clapped and cheered, "Bravo! Jingle your bells, Merry!"

"They love my bells," said Merry to Hairy.

It was Hairy's turn to clown around. Wearing a fluffy orange wig, Hairy honked his horn. He honked as he juggled and honked as he tumbled. The children stood up and roared, "Hooray for Hairy! We want more!"

Hairy triumphantly smiled at Merry and said, "My horn is one big hit."

The circus travelled from town to town, with Merry and Hairy trying new tricks to be better than the other. They bought more and more gadgets for their acts. They even bought their own trailer to carry their props.

Although they were the best of clowns, one day, Merry's biggest fear came true: one of them had to go.

"You are two big clowns in one small circus," said the ringmaster. "You keep getting bigger and bigger. Tonight we'll decide who stays and who goes." He walked away, leaving the two big clowns to think about their "too big" acts.

It was on that night that Merry and Hairy both shrunk and grew. They didn't need to out-do each other. They needed to work as a team. Instead of scheming to be better than the other, Merry and Hairy decided to put their acts together. Now, wherever they go, they perform a two-clown act with jingling bells and honking horns, and are happy to share the spotlight and the applause. And you know what? The children cheer and roar even more.

1. What did Merry do that made her "merry"?

___

2. What did Hairy wear that made him "hairy"?

___

3. What did the ringmaster say one day? Why?

___

___

4. In the end, what did Merry and Hairy decide to do?

___

___

Think!

Merry and Hairy kept trying to be better than each other. They were **rivals**. Look up this word in a dictionary and explain it in your own words. Then think of two rival sports teams that you know about and explain how they are rivals.

"rivals": ____________________

____

Example: ______________ team ______________ team

____

____

B. Use your own words to write the reasons for the following changes in Merry and Hairy.

1. Change: Merry began looking for new things for the clown act.

   Reason: ____________________

2. Change: Merry and Hairy each became "bigger and bigger".

   Reason: ____________________

3. Change: Merry and Hairy decided to work as a team.

   Reason: ____________________

Create a rival of Monster Mike. Draw and describe him or her, and don't forget to give a name. Then write a paragraph about how they went from being rivals to being partners in a team.

Monster Mike

VS.

- funny
- "brainy"
- has strong arms

BOOKS TO READ

Title:
Rivals for the Crown

Author:
Margaret Simpson

Publisher:
Scholastic Children's Books (2003)

Marie's Rating: ★★★★½

"This book took me back to 16th-century England, when Henry VIII was the king. The story is not simply about sibling rivalry – it's about two royal family sisters, Mary and Elizabeth, who had the same father, Henry VIII, but different mothers. Mary felt Elizabeth was the enemy, and Elizabeth felt Mary was hard to deal with. Their family background made their relationship very tense and very complicated. When Mary became Queen of England, Elizabeth was afraid that she would be killed. You have to read this book to find out what happened later in history!"

My Rating: ☆☆☆☆☆

Comments: ______________________________

____

____

____

Checklist

Skills

- ☐ I can identify the two main characters of a story.
- ☐ I know more about the two main characters through Q & A.
- ☐ I understand the meaning of "rivals".
- ☐ I can identify the reasons that make the two main characters change.
- ☐ I know how to create a rival of an imaginary monster and describe how they change from being rivals to being partners.

Revising

- ☐ I have checked my spelling.
- ☐ I have written in complete sentences.

Conflict and Resolution

always involving one or more characters

13

Conflict: The doll and the toymaker have opposite wishes.

In this unit, students will:

- identify sentences that tell opposite things in a story.
- write about the conflict and resolution in the story.
- write their opinions on what happens in the story.
- learn different types of conflict: character against character, character against setting, and character against self.
- describe the conflict and resolution in a picture and write about an example from their lives.

A. Read and look at each coloured sentence. Use the same colour to underline the sentence that tells the opposite.

The Toymaker's Doll

"Her face is so beautiful," the toymaker said of his newest doll. "Her dress is the prettiest I've ever painted. I won't be able to make another doll like this in a hundred years." He decided to keep the doll for himself, and happily placed it on his shelf.

Although the toymaker couldn't let go of the doll, he was not a child, and so did not play with her. The doll sat stiffly, watching her owner whittle and carve, paint and polish. She watched as toys were carefully packed in cartons and carried out the door to a waiting truck.

The doll was not happy to sit on the toymaker's shelf. "I'm young and want to see what is out there in the world," she thought. "If the toymaker sent me to a toy store, I would see beyond this dusty workshop. I would know the warmth of a hug, feel a breeze, or maybe even sit at a tea party." She wished to get out. The toymaker only glanced up at her once in a while, sometimes reaching out to straighten her as she seemed to be slumping a bit.

One day, just as the toymaker was preparing the last carton of toys for delivery to the toy store, he heard a thump behind him. Startled, he whirled around. His beautiful doll lay crumpled in a heap on the floor.

"Oh, you want to go with the others?" the toymaker said, inspecting his fallen toy. He chuckled at his words. "Dolls don't have wishes," he thought. But when he looked at her eyes, they sparkled! She was trying to tell him something. So, the toymaker polished her cheeks and wrapped her in pretty paper. Then into the carton went the doll, and out to the waiting truck she went, all smiles on her face.

B. Write about the conflict and resolution of the story.

1. **Conflict**

   a. the characters involved: ____________________

   b. the conflict: ____________________

   ____

2. **Resolution**

   a. What did the doll do to change her owner's mind?

   ____

   ____

   b. In the end, what did the toymaker do?

   ____

   ____

Think!

____

____

C. Read about these types of conflict. Then identify each one below.

Types of Conflict

character against character

when two characters are in disagreement with each other
e.g. the different wishes between the toymaker and the doll

character against setting

when a character needs to fight against something in nature or society
e.g. harsh winter, racism

character against self

when a character needs to fight against something within himself or herself
e.g. feelings of guilt, anger

1. Sidney must keep his ship afloat in the violent storm.

   ____

2. Sheila and her brother are fighting over who should clean the toilet this weekend.

   ____

3. Rudy must do something to stop his community from closing down the local swimming pool.

   ____

4. Should Amy tell her teacher that her dog really did eat her homework, or should she lie and say that she forgot it?

   ____

Look at this picture. Tell what type of conflict you see and describe it. Look who else is in the picture and write what you think will be the resolution. Then describe an example of conflict and resolution in your life.

Conflict at first base: ____________

____

____

____

____

Resolution: ____________

____

____

Conflict in my life: ____________

____

____

Resolution: ____________

____

____

BOOKS TO READ

Title:
Naomi's Road

Author:
Joy Kogawa

Publisher:
Fitzhenry & Whiteside (2005)

Leo's Rating:

"I like this book because it's written by someone who experienced a huge conflict as a child. In the story, Naomi and her Japanese-Canadian family are taken to an isolated place far from their home because Canada is at war with Japan. Naomi experiences racism not only from the Canadian government, but also from other children."

My Rating:

Comments:

____

____

____

____

Checklist

Skills

- [ ] I can identify sentences that tell opposite things in a story.
- [ ] I can write about the conflict and resolution in the story.
- [ ] I know how to write my opinion on what happens in the story.
- [ ] I understand different types of conflict.
- [ ] I can describe the conflict and resolution in a picture and write about an example from my own life.

Revising

- [ ] I have checked my spelling.
- [ ] I have written in complete sentences.

Plot

pattern of events in a story

14

In this unit, students will:

- learn that "plot" is the pattern of events in a story where the characters try to resolve a conflict.
- learn more about the plot of the story through Q & A.
- identify the type of conflict in the story.
- identify the conflict, events, and resolution in a story with the help of a simple plot diagram.
- find or make up a story with a conflict, events, and a resolution, and make a simple plot diagram.

A. Read the story. Then answer the questions in your own words.

We Are Porpoises!

The tourists were far away. But porpoises hear very, very well, and they knew exactly what the tourists were saying about them.

"Look! A shark fin!" As the boat lingered, the tourists marvelled at the sight of sharks, and then sped off toward shore.

Every porpoise was annoyed. They were proud to be porpoises, but the tourists were always mistaking them for something else.

"We're not sharks. We're porpoises," they said, shaking their stubby heads. "Tomorrow, we'll spout from our blowholes. Sharks don't have blowholes, so that should set the tourists straight."

The next day, another tourist boat slowly approached the waiting pod. Sprays of mist shot up from the porpoises' blowholes. The tourists smiled and pointed. The porpoises listened.

"Look! Whale spouts! Isn't it great to see whales?" The tourists chattered on, admiring what they thought were gigantic whales. Then their boat sped off to see other sights.

Frustrated, the porpoises gathered to make another plan. "We have to get closer to the boat," one said. "If they can see us up close, they will admire us for the porpoises that we are."

The next day, as a tourist boat sputtered to its viewing position, the pod of porpoises swam a little closer. The tourists jumped up and down, pointing. The porpoises listened.

"Look! Dolphins! How wonderful it is to see dolphins!" the tourists said.

Disappointed again, the porpoises swam away. Sure, they were small like dolphins. They had blowholes like whales and triangular dorsal fins like sharks. But they were porpoises! Suddenly, the boat's motor revved. The porpoises decided to play in the waves so that the tourists could see them even better. As they wove in and out, the tourists watched in wonder. They not only saw their fins, their blowholes, and their size, but also their blunt noses and bulky bodies.

The tourists said, "Look! Porpoises! Is there anything more beautiful?" They kept talking. "How fast they swim! How handsome their smiles are!"

And as the porpoises played, they listened, and were very happy.

1. What happened when the porpoises spouted from their blowholes in front of the tourists?

___

2. What did the porpoises do in the end to resolve the conflict?

___

___

3. For the porpoises, what was the most exciting moment? Where is it in the story?

___

___

Think!

Now that you have looked closer at the story, can you identify the type of conflict in it? Fill in the blanks.

Conflict

Type: character against ____________

porpoises against ____________

B. Use your own words to describe the conflict in (A). Then write down the individual events of the story with the help of the plot diagram.

Conflict: The porpoises are proud to be themselves, ____________

____

Events:

Plot Diagram

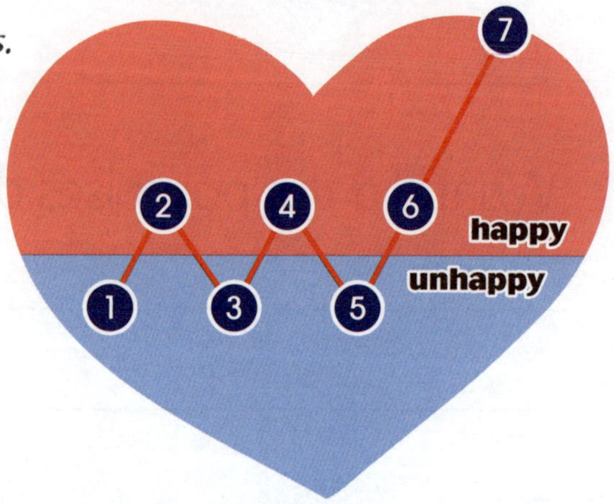

1. *The tourists think the porpoises are sharks.*
2. *The porpoises spout from their blowholes.*
3. *The tourists think the porpoises are whales.*
4. ____________
5. ____________
6. ____________
7. Resolution ____________

Your Turn

Find or make up a story that tells what the conflict is near the beginning. Describe the conflict. Then list the main events and plot them in the ♥ like in (B).

Title: ______________________________

Conflict: ______________________________

____

Plot Diagram

Events:

1 ______________________________

____

2 ______________________________

____

3 ______________________________

4 ______________________________

5 ______________________________

6 ______________________________

7 Resolution ______________________________

BOOKS TO READ

Title:
Beware, Pirates!

Author:
Frieda Wishinsky

Publisher:
Maple Tree Press (2007)

Marie's Rating:

"This book took me back to the time of pirates in Canada's north. Emily and Matt find an old sled that has powers to take them on adventures in the past. They wind up in 1577, exploring the north on Captain Frobisher's ship. The plot moves quickly when they meet an Inuit boy named Minik. They help Minik rescue his friend, who is held captive on Frobisher's ship."

My Rating:

Comments: ______________________________

____

____

____

Checklist

Skills

- [ ] I know that "plot" is the pattern of events in a story.
- [ ] I have learned more about the plot of the story through Q & A.
- [ ] I can identify the type of conflict in the story.
- [ ] I can identify the conflict, events, and resolution in a story with the help of a simple plot diagram.
- [ ] I can find or make up a story with a conflict, events, and a resolution, and make a simple plot diagram.

Revising

- [ ] I have given a title to my story.
- [ ] I have written in complete sentences.

Mysteries

The detective must save the victim!

15

In this unit, students will:

- read a mystery and identify its elements: settings, characters, puzzle, clues, and answer.
- learn some words with similar meanings as "detective", "puzzle", and "clue".
- make an outline of a mystery with the help of a picture and write their own mystery.

A. **Fill in the blanks with "first", "second", "third", and "fourth" to finish this mystery story.**

35 Miller Road

Who would have thought that a nine-year-old like me could solve a crime? Well, that's exactly what I did when I found out where Charlie was trapped and who kidnapped him.

On the ________ day of my newspaper delivery job, my boss Mrs. Grey gave me my paper route and said, "Thirty-five Miller Road is particular about their newspaper delivery. Don't put it in the mailbox, Luke. Just toss it from the road."

At thirty-five Miller Road, you had to unlock an old gate to get to the front door. "So the owner wanted to spare me the trouble," I thought. But I realized it wasn't difficult, so on the ________ day of my job, I decided to put the paper in the mailbox, thinking I would get a tip for doing a good job.

"Thirty-five Miller Road," Mrs. Grey said again on the ________ day, "is particular about their newspaper delivery. Make sure you just toss it from the road." How strange. Didn't the owner appreciate the extra work that I did?

Anyway, I listened. So on the ________ day, I just tossed the paper over the gate. On my way to school, I bumped into my teacher Mr. Brown, and told him that I delivered newspapers every morning. I thought he would be proud of me. "You know, Charlie used to deliver newspapers too," he said, sadly. "I think he even had the same paper route as you. It's too bad that he went missing..."

"Thirty-five Miller Road!" I suddenly thought. "Charlie is probably trapped inside!" No wonder the owner wanted me to stay away from the house. So I rushed to the delivery office to look for Mrs. Grey. She stepped out, but I saw an envelope on the counter addressed to her... at thirty-five Miller Road!

"My boss lives at thirty-five Miller Road!" I said out loud. "She must be the kidnapper!" I grabbed the envelope and dashed to the police station.

Before noon that day, the police came to our school to say that they finally caught Charlie's kidnapper, and that Charlie was safely back home. They also thanked me for helping them solve the case, and gave me an award along with a box of cookies!

B. Write the answers.

1. The two settings of the mystery:

   ____

   ____

2. The detective: ________________

   The victim: ________________

   The villain: ________________

3. The puzzle: ________________________________

4. The answer: ________________________________

C. Check the three clues that helped the detective in (A) solve the mystery.

(A) The owner of 35 Miller Road wanted Luke to stay away from the house.

(B) Mr. Brown had not been going to work in a month.

(C) Charlie used to have the same paper route as Luke.

(D) An envelope addressed to Mrs. Grey showed that she lived at 35 Miller Road.

(E) Charlie's bike was locked outside 35 Miller Road.

Think!

Every mystery story has the following three elements. For each element, underline two other words that have a similar meaning.

Detective	Puzzle	Clue
victim	crime	private eye
private eye	sleuth	hint
villain	suspect	evidence
sleuth	secret	crime

Your Turn

Write a mystery based on this picture. Make an outline first. Then write your story on a lined piece of paper.

Outline of "________________________________"

Setting

Place: ______________________

Time: ______________________

Characters

Detective: ______________________

Victim: ______________________

Villain: ______________________

Puzzle ____

Clues ____

____

Answer ____

THINGS TO TRY

- **Paste a picture of an object on a piece of cardboard.**
- **Cover it with a blank piece of paper. You should be able to "open" the page to look at the picture.**
- **On the blank piece of paper, write a list of clues about what the picture is. Write down your clues below first.**
- **Let your friends guess what's inside. See who takes the shortest time to guess what it is!**

Example:

Clues:

1. Where can you find it? ____________________
2. What colour is it? ____________________
3. How does it sound? ____________________
4. Is it a solid, liquid, or gas? ____________________
5. What is it used for? ____________________

Checklist

Skills

- ☐ I can identify the elements of a mystery.
- ☐ I know some words with similar meanings as "detective", "puzzle", and "clue".
- ☐ I know how to write a mystery with the help of an outline and a picture.

Revising

- ☐ I have filled in all the information in my mystery outline.
- ☐ I have given a title to my mystery.
- ☐ I have written in complete sentences.

16 Formal Letters

Say "thank you" to a museum!

In this unit, students will:

- learn the format of a formal letter and label its different parts.
- read an example of a formal letter and identify its recipient, sender, and purpose.
- think of examples of people and places to whom or which they can write a formal letter.
- tell the features of a formal letter from those of a friendly letter.
- fill in the missing information of a formal letter.

A. Read this formal letter. Then label the different parts with "sender's address", "date", "recipient's address", "salutation", "body", "closing", and "sender".

Coasttown Heights Elementary School
123 Garry Street
Coasttown, BC
V4M 5M6

1. ____________

November 15, 2007

2. ____________

3. ____________

- paragraph 1: words of thanks
- paragraph 2: more detail
- paragraph 3: plans for the near future

Island Museum
456 Oak Street
Coasttown, BC
V1M 2M3

4. ____________

Dear Mr. Castle:

5. ____________ (followed by a colon)

Thank you for the exciting tour at the museum last Friday. Although we have been learning about the medieval times for a few weeks now, it was the museum that brought history to life.

Each of us had a chance to try on the knight's helmet. It was interesting to see the other parts of the armour, too. We were very surprised when one of the arms started to move! It was an excellent trick. We thought that someone must have been in the suit of armour. The best part of the day was seeing how a real trebuchet works. We have decided to build one as a class project.

We are looking forward to another visit to the museum in spring, when we will be learning about the history of our province.

Sincerely,

6. ____________ (followed by a comma)

Mrs. Brown's Grade 4 Class

7. ____________

B. Check each correct answer. Then write down which part of the letter tells you the answer.

1. For whom is the letter?

   (A) Mrs. Brown

   (B) Mr. Castle

   (C) Mrs. Brown's Grade 4 Class

I know this from: ____________________

2. From whom is the letter?

   (A) Mrs. Brown

   (B) Mr. Castle

   (C) Mrs. Brown's Grade 4 Class

I know this from: ____________________

3. Whose address is on the letter?

   (A) the sender's address

   (B) the recipient's address

   (C) the sender's and recipient's addresses

I know this from: ____________________

4. What is the purpose of the letter?

   (A) to tell the parents about the students' museum trip

   (B) to ask the museum about the next trip

   (C) to thank the museum for the museum trip

I know this from: ____________________

Think!

Besides writing a formal letter to thank a museum for a wonderful school trip, we can also write formal letters to these people or places for what they have done for us. Think of a few more examples.

People	Places
school principal	local library
city mayor	the zoo
____________	____________
____________	____________

C. Put these features and uses on the correct types of letter below.

What kind of letter am I if...

- **A** I have the salutation "Hey,"?
- **B** I have the closing "Love,"?
- **C** I have a chatty tone?
- **D** I have a serious tone?
- **E** my purpose is to ask your school to keep the music program?
- **F** my purpose is to say hello to your grandparents?
- **G** I only have one paragraph?

Friendly Letter

Formal Letter

Your Turn

Check what this formal letter has. Then fill in the missing information by making up the date, the salutation, the rest of the second paragraph, and the closing.

Coasttown Heights Elementary School
123 Garry Street
Coasttown, BC
V4M 5M6

____

Island Community Recreation
700 Oak Street
Coasttown, BC
V1M 2M3

____

Thank you for opening a new swimming pool at Island Community Recreation. Thanks to this new pool, our teacher took us swimming for gym class last Tuesday.

We all practised our front crawl and back crawl. Some of us even ____________________

____

____

____

We are looking forward to our next visit to the pool, when we will learn how to dive.

____

Mrs. Brown's Grade 4 Class

Formal Letter Checklist

- [ ] date
- [ ] recipient's name and address
- [ ] salutation
- [ ] body (3 paragraphs)
- [ ] closing
- [ ] sender's name and address

THINGS TO TRY

Steps

1. Cut out 26 small squares from the cardboard of a cereal box.
2. Use a marker to write 26 letters of the alphabet on the 26 squares.
3. Tape the letters to the outside edge of the notebook pages in alphabetical order.
4. Fill the book with addresses of people and places you know (e.g. "Grandma" under "G", "McDonald's" under "M"). First, practise writing an address using this format:

name of person/place: ____________________

street number: ____________________

city, province/territory: ____________________

postal code: ____________________

Checklist

Skills

- ☐ I know the format of a formal letter and I can label its different parts.
- ☐ I can identify the recipient, sender, and purpose of a sample formal letter.
- ☐ I can think of examples of people and places to whom or which I can write a formal letter.
- ☐ I can distinguish between the features of a formal letter and those of a friendly letter.
- ☐ I can fill in the missing information of a formal letter.

Revising

- ☐ I have a colon after the salutation and a comma after the closing.
- ☐ I have used the capital letter in the correct places.

Poems

Does it have rhyming couplets,
or is it in free form?

17

In this unit, students will:

- learn two types of poems: one with rhyming couplets, which has rhyme and rhythm, and one in free form, which has no rhyme or rhythm.
- tell the features of each type of poem by giving an example or a description.
- learn three literary devices (simile, alliteration, personification) and identify examples of each.
- write two different poems about "October", one with rhyming couplets and one in free form.

A. Fill in the blanks with the given words to finish these two poems. Then give an example or a description of their features.

A Poem with Rhyming Couplets

The Pioneer Boy

This is the boy who worked so hard
To help his pa cut wood from the 1. ____________
Who cleared the land of thickets and vines
And brush of all the stubborn 2. ____________

Who planted the seeds and grew the wheat
Who harvested grain in his bare 3. ____________
And saved some for the pigs to eat
To get them fatter so they could give good 4. ____________

And then saved the rest to give to his ma
Who made good bread for him and his 5. ____________
And the rest of the children, the pioneers
Who will do the same for the coming 6. ____________

Features of the poem: *rhyming couplets*

Example: ____

____

A Poem in Free Form

September

pencils
summer
beast
shoes

September

sneaks

c r e e p s

t i p t o e s

cloaked in new 1. ____________ and sharpened 2. ____________

promises a fresh start like the New Year

but it is a 3. ____________

that swallows 4. ____________

Features of the poem:

1. Are there rhyming words? Yes / No
2. Is there rhythm? Yes / No
3. Shape of the words: ______________________________

   ____
4. How the poem looks: ______________________________

   ____

B. Read the meanings of these literary devices. Write "S", "A", or "P" for each sentence below.

We often use literary devices to write poems.

Simile: using the word "like" to compare different things

Alliteration: using the same beginning sound in a series of words

Personification: giving human qualities to an animal, place, or thing

1. September promises a fresh start like the new year. ______
2. Susan saw a silly squirrel scurrying in her yard. ______
3. The cave is yawning on the side of the mountain. ______
4. The cave, like a yawn, gapes on the mountainside. ______
5. Oh no! September has swallowed our summer! ______

Think!

There are five verbs that personify September in the poem "September". They all end in "s". What are they?

______ ______ ______

______ ______

Your Turn

Write two different poems about October, one using rhyming couplets, and one using free form. Use the given words as suggestions. Include the use of simile, alliteration, and/or personification.

October

a poem with rhyming couplets:

witches	princesses	Halloween
Mr. Bean	trick-or-treating	evening

October

a poem in free form:

pumpkins	"Trick or treat!"	costumes
bats	Jack-o'-lanterns	treats

THINGS TO TRY

- **Write a poem about each month on a piece of white paper. Use rhyming couplets or free form.**
- **Paste each poem on a bigger piece of construction paper, punch holes, and tie the pages together with string or yarn.**
- **First, make a plan of what type of poem you will write for each month.**

My Plan

January	____________		
February	____________		
March	____________		
April	____________		
May	____________	June	____________
July	____________	August	____________
September	____________	October	____________
November	____________	December	____________

Checklist

Skills

- ☐ I have learned two types of poems: one with rhyming couplets and one in free form.
- ☐ I can identify rhyming couplets and I can describe the appearance of a poem in free form.
- ☐ I can identify examples of simile, alliteration, and personification.
- ☐ I know how to write a poem with rhyming couplets and a poem in free form.

Revising

- ☐ I can hear the rhythm in my poem with rhyming couplets.
- ☐ I have used rhyming words in my poem with rhyming couplets.

News Articles

Find out what's going on!

18

In this unit, students will:

- read a news article and identify its features.
- learn what the article is about by answering the five W-questions: Who, What, When, Where, Why.
- put missing quotation marks in examples of direct speech.
- give an opinion based on facts in the article.
- write a news article using a template.

A. Read this news article. Then identify the features of the article by writing the numbers in the circles on the next page.

1 Thursday, July 5, 2007

2

Alligator gone from zoo!

3 **By Wendy Sharma**
staff reporter

An alligator, missing from his pen at the Sea City Zoo since yesterday morning, has nearby residents afraid to leave their homes. Police, animal control officers, and many volunteers are trying to locate the reptile.

4 "This is not like Albert," said Sam Longfoot, the alligator's keeper. "He has a great home here at the zoo. I only left the gate open for a minute while I cleaned his pen, which I do every week."

A long-time zoo resident, the alligator was well-fed at the zoo. According to Longfoot, his diet of fresh duck was recently upgraded to fresh turkey. "He loves duck, but we thought it was time for a change," said Longfoot. He and other zoo workers have been keeping a round-the-clock watch for the gator.

Police believe that the alligator may be in the neighbourhood between the Sea City Zoo and the Duck Pond. He is black, about four metres long, with a wide snout. While alligators are generally shy of people, police ask that children and pets be kept inside. All residents are advised to be cautious until the alligator is found.

5

6 Alligator Albert was last seen at the zoo the day before yesterday.

Features of a News Article

- ◯ headline
- ◯ date
- ◯ photo
- ◯ byline
- ◯ speech
- ◯ caption

B. Read what Albert says and answer the questions below.

Now that you know the features of a news article, it's time to tell what the article is about using the **five Ws**.

1. **Who** is the article about?

 ____

2. **What** happened to him or her?

 ____

3. **When** did it happen?

 ____

4. **Where** did it happen?

 ____

5. **Why** did it happen?

 ____

C. Reporter Wendy Sharma went out to the streets to find out what people say about the missing alligator. Put quotation marks around the direct speech.

1. The owner of a local market excused himself, saying, I've got to check my meat department!

2. Great. Gators! What next? said a resident of Waterfront Retirement Homes.

3. I guess I won't be able to see Albert for a while, said Tom, sadly. Tom loves reptiles and visits Albert at the Sea City Zoo every week.

4. The children of Mallard Elementary School were ecstatic when they were told to stay at home until the alligator was back at the zoo. They are happy to miss their math quiz, said Mr. Drake, a grade four teacher.

Think!

Why do you think Albert escaped from the zoo? Give facts from the news article to support your answer.

____

____

____

____

The alligator has been found! Write a news article about it. Make up the missing features of the article. Remember to include information that tells the five Ws.

By ____________________

staff reporter

Albert has just finished his lunch back at the Sea City Zoo.

THINGS TO TRY

- **Find an article from the newspaper.**
- **Make a checklist of its features (it may have some or all of the features below).**
- **Write down the information from the article on the lines.**

☐ Date: ____________________

☐ Headline: ____

☐ Byline: ____________________

____

☐ Photo

☐ Caption: ____

____

☐ Speech: ____

____

____

Checklist

Skills

☐ I know the features of a news article and I can identify them.

☐ I can find out what an article is about by answering the five W-questions: Who, What, When, Where, Why.

☐ I know how to show direct speech using quotation marks.

☐ I know how to make an opinion based on facts from the article.

☐ I know how to write a news article using a template.

Revising

☐ My article has a headline.

☐ I have included information that tells the five Ws in my article.

ANSWERS

ANSWERS

1 Nouns

A. Underline these words in bold:
llamas ;
dollars ; friends ; herd ;
apples ; treat ;
horses ; family ;
jackets ;
animals

B. 1. love 2. attention
3. happiness 4. fur
5. water 6. hay
7. daylight 8. air
9. grass 10. land

Think!
1. rooms ; room
2. joy ; joys

C. 1. ✘
2. ✘
3. ✔
4. ✔

Corrections
1 ; Lou's wife made too many jackets for him.
2 ; There are too few treats for the llamas today.

D. 1. many 2. little
3. much 4. few

Your Turn
Countable Nouns:
one big bowl ; one spoon ; two eggs ; four cookie cutters
Uncountable Nouns:
a bag of flour ; a tub of butter ; a carton of milk
1. two eggs, a bag of flour, a tub of butter, and a carton of milk
2. a big bowl, a spoon, and four different cookie cutters

2 Compound Words

A. Underline these words in bold:
butterfly ; honeybee ; hummingbird ; nothing ; breakfast ;
ladybug ; grasshopper ; bulldog ;
skateboard ; sidewalk ; policewoman ; everybody ; bookkeeper ; nobody ;
butterflies ; flowerpot

B. 1. bulldog
2. butterfly
3. skateboard
4. grass ; hopper
5. humming ; bird
6a. breakfast
b. sidewalk
c. flowerpot

Think!
1. cup ; board ; cupboard
2. sand ; box ; sandbox

C. (In any order)
catfish ; sandpaper ; toothpaste ; grandmother ; footprint ; popcorn
(Individual writing of the sentence)

Your Turn
cowboy ; horseback ; raincoat ; rainbow ; sandbox ; sunshine
(Suggested writing)
A cowboy on horseback is taking off his raincoat because the rain has stopped. There is now sunshine and a rainbow in the sky. The cowboy's dog is playing in the sandbox.

3 Verbs

A. Underwater: B
On Land: A
Underground: B
In the Air: B

B. 1. They will amble out of the pond.
2. They will snatch them up.

C.

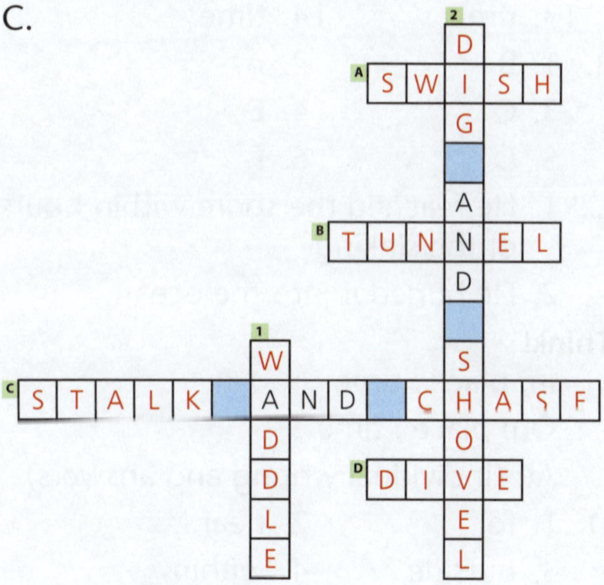

D. 1. will practise
2. will plant
3. shape
4. will travel
5. will dart

Think!

- Carly will swim five laps around the pool.
- Carly is going to swim five laps around the pool.

Your Turn

1. will spin towards the ground to be carried by wind
2. will float to their new home
3. will carry them away
4. will come off the plant and hitch a ride

4 Adjectives

A. Quebec:
biggest ; colder
New Brunswick:
highest ; more amazing
Alberta:
most westerly ; sunniest
Prince Edward Island:
most rural ; smallest ; more relaxed

B. 1. smaller
2. colder
3. bigger
4. higher

C. 1a. snowier ; snowiest
b. busier ; busiest
c. sunnier ; sunniest
2. sunnier
3. snowier
4. busiest

D. 1a. more beautiful ; most beautiful
b. more westerly ; most westerly
c. more ancient ; most ancient
d. more rural ; most rural
2. most rural
3. most beautiful
4. more westerly
5. most ancient

Think!

1. worse
2. most

Your Turn

1. Prince Edward Island is smaller than Nova Scotia.
2. Nunavut is bigger than Manitoba.
3. Ontario is wider than British Columbia.
4. Saskatchewan is narrower than Alberta.

5. Yukon is the most westerly territory of Canada.
6. Newfoundland and Labrador is the most easterly province of Canada.

5 Adverbs

A. Underline these words:
politely ; diligently ; happily ; immediately ;
urgently ; wisely ;
neatly ; busily ; freshly ; tightly ; proudly ;
eagerly ; slowly ; suspiciously ; completely

B. 1. She does her homework diligently.
2. They climb up the stairs eagerly.
3. It has completely transformed.

C. 1. quickly
2. loosely
3. rudely
4. lightly/casually

Think!
(Individual answers)

D. 1. bravely ; carefully ;
easily ; awkwardly ;
sloppily ; wonderfully ;
cheerily ; carelessly
2. easily
3. bravely
4. carefully ; carelessly
5. wonderfully ; sloppily
6. awkwardly ; cheerily

Your Turn
(Individual answers and writing)

6 Prepositions

A. 1. direction 2. place
3. time 4. time
5. time 6. place
7. time 8. time
9. time 10. place
11. direction 12. direction
13. time 14. time

B. 1. B 2. A
3. C 4. E
5. D 6. F

C. 1. He reached the shore within hours of the sinking.
2. He hurled it into the ocean.

Think!
In: place ; time
On: place ; time
At: (Individual writing and answers)

D. 1. for 2. near
3. outside 4. within
5. into 6. to
7. from

Your Turn
(Individual writing)

7 Conjunctions

A. Underline these conjunctions throughout the passage:
because ; so ; if ; until ; since ; while ; although

B. 1. while others find dinosaur teeth or dung
2. until they are as hard as rocks
3. because we can learn a lot from footprints

Think!

1. Janet is excited to find a dinosaur head because/since she has never seen a dinosaur fossil.
2. Janet and Bill are going home because/since they have finished their work today.

C. 1. you are interested in dinosaurs.
2. You might be able to find a dinosaur fossil if you live where dinosaurs used to roam.
3. Dinosaur fossils are quite rare although fossils of one kind or another can be common.
4. Minerals seep into holes in the buried animal bones since the minerals that form rock are also in the water.

Your Turn

(Individual answers and writing)

8 Sentences

A. Zoo Rules

Do not feed the animals or put your fingers through the fences.

Eat only in areas with a sign because it is important to keep the zoo clean.

Animal Viewing

If they are not in the viewing area, just come back later.

Donations

We want to protect endangered species, but we can do so only with your help.

Your donations will go toward habitat rebuilding and they will help fund our zoo programs, so your help is very important to us.

Parking

If you want to park your car and then use the nearby subway, you should use the pay parking lot beside the subway station.

B. 1. Any one of these:

Stay behind the yellow line.

Balloons are not allowed in the zoo.

Some of the animals take a mid-day nap in their shelters.

All zoo visitors park for free.

Free parking is for zoo visitors only.

2. 2 ; or
3. 4 ; because
4. Your donations will go toward habitat rebuilding and they will help fund our zoo programs, so your help is very important to us.

Think!

1. compound
2.
3.
4. compound

C. (Suggested writing)

1. Michael wants to see the boa constrictor because he loves all kinds of reptiles. ; complex
2. Dave is down with a cold, so he can't go to see the zebras. ; compound
3. Mrs. Lee can take her kids to the zoo every week this summer because she bought a zoo pass. ; complex
4. Jodi loves animals and she wants to make a donation, but the zoo is closed for a month. ; compound

Your Turn

(Suggested writing)

1. Ben is climbing a tree because he wants to be a monkey.

ANSWERS

2. Dan is pointing at the giraffes and they smile back at him.
3. The zookeeper looks on while Bill is making a funny face.
4. Bill is making a funny face but the lion is not paying attention.
5. Erica has a banana, so she is giving it to a monkey.
6. Lisa can feed the elephant a banana or she can feed carrots.

9 Punctuation

A. In the time of kings and castles, it was common for a boy to dream of becoming a knight. The trouble with Norman, who wanted to be a knight, was that he wasn't a boy. Norman was a newt.

Norman scrabbled to a castle near the pond where he was born. At the gate, he said to the guards, "I want to be a knight."

"How can a newt be a knight?" asked one of the guards. "A newt lives in the marshes." The guard stomped his foot and called to the others, "This newt is a nut! Close the gate!"

Disappointed, Norman went home. Before long, his wish to be a knight took him back to the castle. This time, he bumped into some knights on their way to a tournament. He said, "I want to be a knight like you."

One of the knights laughed and said, "A newt is only a threat to insects and worms, not knights from other kingdoms." The knight raised his sword and said, "This newt is a hoot! Onward, knights!"

Norman would have to go straight to the king. He squeezed under the gate, crawled past the guards, and wriggled up the wall to an open window. What luck! He was in the throne room, and there was the king, polishing his golden crown.

"Your Majesty," Norman said quickly before the king could call his guards, "I want to be a knight. Knights must fight for their king, so I'm perfect for the job. After all, I eat dragonflies!"

The king didn't know much about newts, nor did he know anything about dragonflies, but it certainly sounded brave to eat them. And so, by order of the king, Norman the newt became a knight!

Think!

1. At the gate, he said to the guards, "I want to be a knight."
2. "How can a newt be a knight?" asked one of the guards.

B. 1. The guard said, "This newt is a nut!"
2. The knight said, "This newt is a hoot!"
3. The king said, "This newt is brave!"

C. 1. Norman eats dragonflies!
2. Norman eats dragonflies?
3. Norman eats dragonflies.

Your Turn

1. The king said, "This newt will become a knight."
2. The guard said, "Are you sure about it?"
3. The knight said, "Norman is much smaller than all of us."
4. Norman said, "I will learn to slay real dragons!"

Review

A. 1. animals
2. bacon
3. web
4. bedtime
5. confidence
6. himself
7. eggs
8. lifespan
9. love
10. loyalty
11. friendship

B. 1. animals, web, eggs, lifespan, friendship
2. bacon, confidence, love, loyalty
3. bedtime, himself, lifespan, friendship
4. lifespan, friendship

C. 1. will die ; will save ; will spin ; will want
2. will guide ; will be
3. will take ; will win
4. will return ; will look after
5. (Individual answer)

D. 1. kindest ; kindly
2. most patient ; patiently
3. busier ; busily
4. more independent ; independently

E. 1. inside
2. since
3. before
4. outside
5. near
6. from
7. to
8. after

F. (Individual writing and answers)

G. Shortly before Charlotte dies at the county fair, she says to Wilbur, "A spider's life can't help being something of a mess, with all the trapping and catching flies. By helping you, perhaps I was trying to lift up my life a trifle."

10 Theme

A. B

B. 1. found
2. thought
3. hid
4. wondered
5. realized
6. went

C. (Suggested answers)
1. She realized that someone must be looking for the missing necklace, so she should not keep it.
2. She was happy about her decision in the end because she skipped home, smiling.
3. (Individual writing)

Think!
(Individual answers)

Your Turn
(Individual writing)

11 Setting

A. 1. The story took place in a quiet neighbourhood.
The boys now reached their tree-lined street of comfortable homes.
2. It took place in the fall.
Halloween was coming up and they wanted to do a scary project.

ANSWERS

3. It was late afternoon.

   "How about a haunted house?" Marcus asked, shading his eyes from the late afternoon sun.

Think!

- The attic had a broken window.
- The house was strangely dark against the clear blue sky.
- It had a roof so pointed that it seemed to pierce the sky.
- There were two dead trees with bare branches.

B. 1. shuffled ; hear
2. sweet ; smell
3. roasted ; taste
4. bats ; see
5. squeak ; hear
6. broken ; pointed ; dead ; see
7. chills ; feel

Your Turn

(Individual writing)

12 Characters

A. 1. She jingled the bells on her shoes.
2. He wore a fluffy orange wig.
3. He said that one of them had to go because they were too big for his small circus.
4. They decided to stop out-doing each other and work as a team instead.

Think!

(Individual answers)

B. 1. A new clown named Hairy joined the circus.
2. They wanted to be better than each other.
3. They were each too big for the small circus.

Your Turn

(Individual drawing and writing)

13 Conflict and Resolution

A. The doll was not happy to sit on the toymaker's shelf.

"Dolls don't have wishes," he thought.

B. 1a. the toymaker and his doll
b. The toymaker wanted to keep the doll in his workshop, but the doll wanted to see the world.
2a. Her eyes sparkled when the toymaker asked if she wanted to go with the other toys onto the truck.
b. He polished the doll's cheeks and wrapped her in pretty paper to be delivered to the toy store.

Think!

(Individual answer)

C. 1. character against setting
2. character against character
3. character against setting
4. character against self

Your Turn

(Individual writing)

14 Plot

A. 1. The tourists thought they were whales.
2. The porpoises played in the waves so that the tourists could see their fins, blowholes, size, blunt noses, and bulky bodies.

3. The most exciting moment for the porpoises was when the tourists finally realized that they were porpoises. It is at the end of the story.

Think!

character ; tourists

B. Conflict:

but the tourists always mistake them for something else.

Events:

4. The porpoises swim closer to the tourist boat.
5. The tourists think the porpoises are dolphins.
6. The porpoises decide to play in the waves.
7. The tourists finally see that the animals are porpoises.

Your Turn

(Individual writing)

15 Mysteries

A. first ; second ; third ; fourth

B. 1. Mrs. Grey's office and 35 Miller Road
2. Luke ; Charlie ; Mrs. Grey
3. Charlie is missing.
4. Mrs. Grey is the kidnapper.

C. A ; C ; D

Think!

Detective: private eye ; sleuth

Puzzle: crime ; secret

Clue: hint ; evidence

Your Turn

(Individual writing)

16 Formal Letters

A. 1. sender's address
2. date
3. body
4. recipient's address
5. salutation
6. closing
7. sender

B. 1. B ; the salutation
2. C ; the sender
3. C ; the sender's and recipient's addresses
4. C ; the body

Think!

(Individual answers)

C. Friendly Letter: A ; B ; C ; F ; G

Formal Letter: D ; E

Your Turn

(Individual writing)

17 Poems

A. A Poem with Rhyming Couplets:

1. yard
2. kinds
3. feet
4. meat
5. pa
6. years

Example: (Any of the first two or the last two lines of each stanza)

A Poem in Free Form:

1. shoes
2. pencils
3. beast
4. summer

Features of the poem:

1. No
2. No
3. The fonts of some of the words show the meaning of the words.
4. The lines are not lined up.

B. 1. P / S
2. A
3. P
4. S / P
5. P

Think!

sneaks ; creeps ; tiptoes ; promises ; swallows

Your Turn

(Individual writing)

18 News Articles

A. headline: 2
date: 1
photo: 5
byline: 3
speech: 4
caption: 6

B. 1. It is about an alligator named Albert.
2. He went missing.
3. It happened on July 4, 2007.
4. It happened at the Sea City Zoo.
5. The gate was left open for a minute while the alligator's keeper cleaned the pen.

C. 1. The owner of a local market excused himself, saying, "I've got to check my meat department!"
2. "Great. Gators! What next?" said a resident of Waterfront Retirement Homes.
3. "I guess I won't be able to see Albert for a while," said Tom, sadly. Tom loves reptiles and visits Albert at the Sea City Zoo every week.
4. The children of Mallard Elementary School were ecstatic when they were told to stay at home until the alligator was back at the zoo. "They are happy to miss their math quiz," said Mr. Drake, a grade four teacher.

Think!

(Individual answer)

Your Turn

(Individual writing)